Waterford City

CIAN MANNING

Waterford City

—

A HISTORY

Front cover illustration: Van der Hagen's 'View of Waterford', 1736 (Waterford Treasures)
Back cover illustration: view of Waterford from the north-west, County Waterford *c.* 1890–1900 (Library of Congress)

First published 2019

The History Press
97 St George's Place, Cheltenham,
Gloucestershire, GL50 3QB
www.thehistorypress.co.uk

© Cian Manning, 2019

The right of Cian Manning to be identified as the Author of this work has been asserted in accordance with the Copyright, Designs and Patents Act 1988.

All rights reserved. No part of this book may be reprinted or reproduced or utilised in any form or by any electronic, mechanical or other means, now known or hereafter invented, including photocopying and recording, or in any information storage or retrieval system, without the permission in writing from the Publishers.

British Library Cataloguing in Publication Data.
A catalogue record for this book is available from the British Library.

ISBN 978 1 8458 8909 8

Typesetting and origination by The History Press
Printed and bound by TJ International Ltd

CONTENTS

	Acknowledgements	7
	Introduction: Waterford, its Historians and Historiography	9
1	*Vedrafjordr*: Viking Waterford	15
2	A Royal City: Anglo-Norman Waterford	34
3	*Urbs Intacta Manet Waterfordia*: Late Medieval Waterford	51
4	*Parva Roma* – Little Rome: Waterford in the Sixteenth and Seventeenth Centuries	62
5	The Crystal City: Eighteenth-Century Waterford	84
6	Waterford in the Long Nineteenth Century	104
7	From Here to Modernity: Twentieth-Century Waterford	155
	Epilogue	203
	Bibliography	206

ACKNOWLEDGEMENTS

Over the course of researching and writing *Waterford City: A History* for The History Press, I've been fortunate to have met many erudite, obliging, encouraging and kind people. I would like to begin by thanking Nicola Guy of The History Press for all her help throughout the process of putting this book together and for being beyond generous in her support and advice.

A great deal of thanks goes to the Waterford Archaeological and Historical Society from whom this opportunity arose, with special thanks to Beatrice Payet, Ann Cusack, Erica Fay, Tony Gunning, Michael Maher, Donnchadh Ó Ceallachain and Clare Walsh for all their words of encouragement and for their willingness to listen and give a young person a chance to express their viewpoint. The society is a fantastic community of people who have a great love for history and that of the city of Waterford; it is one of the unsung organisations in our city and county that continues to go from strength to strength.

Thanks to Willie Fraher and all of Waterford County Museum for their help in relation to images. My gratitude to Joanne Rothwell of the Waterford City and County Archives for her help, advice and pointers throughout the process of putting this publication together. This can be clearly seen in the wonderful maps which illustrate this study. My appreciation also to Waterford Treasures, to its director Eamonn McEneaney, with particular reference to Donnchadh Ó Ceallachain (yes, the same person as named with the Waterford Archaeological and Historical Society) for all their help and pointers. Donnchadh is without doubt the most unsung person in the pursuit and promotion of the history of Waterford. He has always been kind to give his time and knowledge when approached about any aspect of history. Donnchadh may not have been born or bred in Waterford but it is a privilege that our city can count him among one of its champions.

A word of thanks to my friends Tracey Bradfield, Barry Condon, Daniel Collins, Tomas de Paor, Bart Gozdur, Gavin King (and his car Betsy for our frequent journeys across the island and the necessary break from writing), Maria-Assunta Lawton, Aisling McDonald, Ann-Marie Keating, David Robson, Rina Ryan, Joanne Tuohy and Eoin Walsh. I am honoured to call them my friends and can only be indebted to them for putting up with my antics. Particular thanks to Gavin, Tomas and Eoin who frequently listened to me discuss my progress with this book.

A great deal of gratitude to Peigí Devlin for all her time, help and expertise with the process of writing this book. Always generous with her time and opinions, this study would not have come to completion without her help and encouragement. It is a better work because of her input, and that is greatly appreciated.

Thanks also are due to Laura O'Brien and Mount Sion Primary School where, over the course of writing this book, I was able to present some of my research to several 5th classes. It was with great pride that I could return to my old school and meet some articulate and mannerly young men. It is safe to say with the pupils of Mount Sion's love of the history of the city that the future of the city is safe in their hands.

Special mention for Grace and Dara Cunningham, Ben Penkert and Leia Murphy, Noah, Arwyn and Hugo Farrell and Lily Guidera for their part on the journey in writing this book.

I would like to thank my aunts Bennie Flynn and Elizabeth Foskin as well as my uncles Liam and Raymond Murphy for all their help over the years.

Thanks to my parents Oliver and Miriam Manning for their continued support and encouragement in all my endeavours. My interest in history and love of Waterford comes from both of them. My effort is always to try and measure up to the Manning motto of 'to be rather than seem to be', and teaching me to be myself has been the greatest lesson, one which I'm still learning with their help.

Thanks to my brother Olin who has always been a great sounding board for ideas and projects. Always one to express an opinion about what is interesting or isn't, a lot of this book was written with him in mind.

INTRODUCTION:
Waterford, its Historians and Historiography

*I have given up doubt,
That old, worn out coat.
All that's constant
Is the fact of change;
Pearl of love, grit of pain.*

Sean Dunne, 'Letter to Lisbon', *Time and the Island* (1996)

The year 1746 is the foundation stone in the history of writing the story of Waterford. A Dungarvan doctor, Charles Smith, was the pioneer in recording the narrative of Waterford to that point and set a template which others have continued to follow to this day. Smith was a forerunner of Irish topography and local history. His collaboration with Walter Harris and Hans Sloane on *The Antient and Present State of the County of Down* preceded his work on Waterford by two years as the first in-depth history of an Irish county. This was followed by similar works on Cork and Kerry for the Physico-Historical Society, Dublin, which were advertised to wealthy individuals of the upper classes interested in improving their knowledge of Irish history.

Prior to the twentieth century, there were four histories of the county, three by men from Dungarvan (Smith in 1746, Ryland in 1824 and Hansard in 1870) while the quartet is completed by P.M. Egan (1894) of Kilkenny. Thus, with this in mind, The History Press Ireland has sought a history devoted specifically to the City of Waterford. In addition, it is worth keeping in view the characteristics and skills of these authors. Julian Walton writes that Ryland 'certainly had his limitations; he lacked Smith's painstaking if pedantic scholarship and Egan's exuberant accumulation of detail'. It just demonstrates the difficult task to write a detailed, authoritative history.

Variation in approach can be seen with M.J. Hurley's *Links and Landmarks being a Calendar for the year 1900, recording curious and remarkable events in the History of Waterford City from the earliest times to the present day*, which sought to cover anniversaries of historical events over the course of a calendar year, and which was published in 1900.

In 1914, Edmund Downey published his history of the city (re-published in 1932) followed by a work on the county by Canon Power in 1932 (re-published in 1937 and 1952). Downey is best described as a 'Man of Letters' since he was editor of London's *Tinsley's* magazine, then started his own publishing company printing Irish classics and his own works under the pseudonym 'F.M. Allen'. His *Illustrated guide to Waterford* provided interesting biographical entries of accomplished (and not so acclaimed but noteworthy) inhabitants of the city.

View of Waterford from the north-west, County Waterford, Ireland, *c.* 1890–1900. *Library of Congress*

Introduction: Waterford, its Historians and Historiography

The latter man, Canon Power, of all the individuals outlined has probably left the greatest lasting impact. At University College Cork, Power held the Chair of Archaeology for nearly twenty years (1915–32). He was ordained in 1885 and began his parish work in Liverpool and subsequently New South Wales, Australia. Power returned to his hometown of Waterford, which coincided with the foundation of the Waterford and South-East Ireland Archaeological Society in 1894. He was a prolific writer, with his impressive recording of the place names of Waterford and around thirty other works from pamphlets to books. His 1907 *Placenames of the Decies* has been well thumbed by local historians and referred to continually by studies on Waterford, it has served as a template to anyone who would undertake such a momentous task.

Another marvel of his work is the *Canon Power Memorial Map of County Waterford and Environs* produced in 1953 by the County Waterford National Monuments Advisory Committee, which he chaired from 1931. Canon Power was described by Lawrence William White and Aideen Foley as 'gentle and unworldly, with an old-word courtesy, Power was tirelessly devoted to his research'. The tradition that began upon Power's return to Waterford with the *Journal of the Waterford and South-East Archaeological Society* continues to this day with its successor of the Waterford Archaeological and Historical Society's *Decies*.

Another very important marker in the historiography of Waterford was the publication of *Waterford: History and Society* in 1992 under the stewardship of Des Cowman, Dr William Nolan and Dr Thomas Power as part of the county-by-county history series undertaken by University College Dublin. This interdisciplinary approach covered various facets of history encompassing archaeology and folklore to arrive at a broader understanding of the county's experience through the centuries.

Two years prior to *Waterford: History and Society* was the publication of Patrick C. Power's *History of Waterford City and County* in 1990. Significant works to have been published in more recent times include *The Royal Charters of Waterford* by Julian Walton in 1992 and *Waterford Treasures* by Eamonn McEneaney in 2004.

The level of recording the history in words is reflected equally in the process of preserving and displaying precious artefacts that illustrate the rich history of Waterford, while bringing to life the story and development of the city we live in today. In 1835, Thomas Wyse, MP For Waterford, sought for the government of the day to support the construction of a building 'for the ordinary objects of an institute, a museum and a gallery of design' at a meeting in the Assembly Rooms, City Hall.

In 1897, the Waterford and South-East Archaeological Society started a small museum in the city at the free library at No. 1 Adelphi Terrace (where the Tower Hotel is now situated) like that of the Science and Art Museum in Dublin where visitors could 'inspect a collection of objects equal to any in Ireland', as recorded in the group's annual reports. By the early twentieth century, the museum moved to Lady Lane before settling at Reginald's Tower in 1954 after the interior of the tower was modified to become a museum. At this time the collection was larger, with additions from Canon Power and the municipal collection to draw upon.

The archaeological excavations of the late 1980s and early '90s in the development of the City Square Shopping Centre saw many of the artefacts found displayed in Reginald's Tower. These items were transferred to the Methodist Church at Greyfriars Street, which was acquired by the council in 1988 to be refashioned as a museum to display the significant findings of the excavations in Waterford City (until 1999).

The 1990s saw conservation work on Reginald's Tower (work starting in 1993) and the conversion of the Granary building on Hanover Street into a museum beginning in 1997. This led to the opening of Waterford Museum of Treasures in 1999, with the director of the museum, Eamonn McEneaney, outlining that 'central to our philosophy in developing the exhibition was that the collection be accessible and welcoming to the public ... On an intellectual level every effort had been made to appeal to as broad an audience as possible.'

Further development has seen Waterford Treasures move from Hanover Street to the Viking Triangle area in the creation of Ireland's first museum quarter. Reginald's Tower serves to showcase the history of Viking Waterford, the Bishop's Palace has been converted into a museum displaying the history of the Georgian period to more modern times (opened in 2011), and the Medieval Museum, Ireland's only purpose-built museum dedicated to the Middle Ages, was opened to the public in 2012. As our historical understanding continues to grow it is continually being matched by our thirst for

Introduction: Waterford, its Historians and Historiography

knowledge, which is mirrored in the developments of these award-winning museums that cater proudly and boldly for all ages.

Now into the eleventh century of Waterford City, books published on the city's history are more numerous, more colourfully illustrated and increasingly beginning to deal with a wider range of subjects compared to the staid 'great men' of history ethos. Such studies include Emmet O'Connor's *A Labour history of Waterford* (1989) to more personal and anecdotal histories such as *Ballybricken and Thereabouts, Waterford and Thereabouts* and *Reminiscences of Waterford* which all appeared in the last decade of the twentieth century, they are thoroughly enlightening and highly engaging histories.

Medieval Museum in Waterford is Ireland's first purpose-built museum dedicated to the Middle Ages. The gable end depicts an image from a belt mount dating to 1250. It may be a representation of Saint Margaret holding the head of a dragon which she has slain. *Courtesy of Waterford Treasures*

Works such as Julian Walton's publicly adored *On This Day* radio slot (with selected episodes published to mark the 1,100th Anniversary of the establishment of the city in 2014) to Colm Long's *Random Waterford History* (published in 2013) evoke much of our present tastes while allude to our historical forebearers such as Hurley's calendar of 1900.

As Julian Walton, an eminent local historian, notes:

> The local historian might keep these in mind. All great events have a local beginning or a local dimension. What happened locally may have been the seeds or the mirrors of revolutions, the fall of dynasties, or a cultural renaissance.

In the words of Waterford poet Sean Dunne, 'All's that constant / Is the fact of change', which is reflected in the studies on the city. It can be explored in the make-up of those who wrote such histories being exclusively men with the strong presence of religion, such as in the careers of Reverend Ryland and Canon Power influencing their subject matter. If ever the writing of history is symptomatic of the times in which it is written, it can be seen in the historiography of the city of Waterford.

In twenty-first-century Waterford, the city is more than adequately catered for with academic historians, modern museums and an ease of access to information that has never previously existed. The Internet, with online platforms or social media groups such as the Waterford History Group, has allowed history to become an increasingly engaging and reachable subject for ordinary members of the public. There are various oral history projects that have documented childhood in Barrack Street, adolescent experiences in the Savoy or Regal Cinemas, schooling at Mount Sion, to courting in John's Park. These not only serve to record the idiosyncrasies of Waterford City but also the universality of experience that we can all relate to. Over the centuries, the people of Waterford have had to overcome everything from Anglo-Norman invaders and English conquerors to the Bubonic Plague and famine, while also trying to deal with, as Dunne wrote, a 'Pearl of love, grit of pain'. The universality of human experience is the same even if the context of time and place are different. It's a familiar story with different settings.

This book is *Waterford City: A History* and serves to explore the story of the city and its people, from poets and scholastic prelates to pop-stars and soccer players. It is very much a potted look at important events in the life of the city, encompassing Viking marauders to Anglo-Norman invaders and the development of Waterford's economy and civic governance. Various figures and personalities are explored which have left an impact on the city and further afield. A history of any area and its people will have omissions or certain aspects perhaps not covered in the depth desired, but I hope, in the words written here, that the love of my city comes across. You, the reader, will be the judge of that.

1

VEDRAFJORDR:
Viking Waterford

TIMELINE

853 CE: Charles Smith's *The Ancient and Present State of the County and City of Waterford* notes that the foundation of Waterford by the Viking King *Sitricus* in CE 853.

914 CE: Deemed to be the most credible date for the foundation of Waterford by archaeologists and historians, with the Viking Ragnall establishing a *longphort* that formed the basis for Waterford City.

921 CE: Ragnall dies as the King of York and Waterford. He captured York (or *Jorvik*) the most significant city in the Viking world in CE 918.

1031 CE: Waterford is scorched to the ground. Six years later, the King of Leinster, Diarmuid Mac Maol na mBó, burnt the city in CE 1037. Just over fifty years later, in CE 1088, Waterford was destroyed by a fire started by the Vikings of Dublin.

1088 CE: A slaughtering of the Vikings who had settled at Waterford was carried out by the Irish and is detailed in *The Annals of the Four Masters* (which was compiled between 1632 and 1636).

1096 CE: Malchus is consecrated the first Bishop of Waterford by Anselm, the Archbishop of Canterbury.

1111 CE: Fire destroys Waterford, with the probable cause believed to be lighting.

1137 CE: The King of Leinster, Diarmuid Mac Murchadha, attempts to capture Waterford. Failing, he starts a fire which burns the city.

1170 CE: Waterford is captured by Richard de Clare, the Earl of Pembroke (also known as Strongbow). He marries the King of Leinster's daughter Aoife in Christ Church Cathedral in the city.

Port Lairge. This is the ancient and present Irish name of the city of Waterford. It would appear to have derived this name from a Danish chieftain Lairge or Larac, or as the Danes write it Largo, who is mentioned in the Annals of the Four Masters at the year 951. The name Waterford or Vedrafiordr, was given it by the Danes; which is supposed to signify 'weather bay.'

From *The genealogy of Corca Laidhe* (Author: Unknown), p.153

THE DANES OF WATERFORD

Like golden-belted bees about a hive
Which come forever and forever go
Going and coming with the ebb and flow,
From year to year, the strenuous Ostman strive.

Close in their billow-battling galleys prest,
Backhands and forwards with the trusty tide
They sweep and wheel around the ocean wide,
Like eagles swooping from their cliff-built nests.

And great their joy, returning where they left
Their tricorned stronghold by the Suirshore
'Mid song and feast, to tell their exploits o'er –
Of all the helm-like glibs their swords had cleft,
The black-haired damsels seized, the towers attacked.
The still monastic cities they had sucked.

St John's Manor House, 17 September 1874

VIKINGS: FROM RAIDERS TO SETTLERS, WOODSTOWN TO WATERFORD

The narrative of Waterford starts in the Viking Age, the period which saw Norse raiders plunder the island of Ireland from the eighth century and gradually settling by the eleventh century. First arriving in Ireland in 795, in the subsequent centuries the Vikings established what are today the island's oldest cities and towns. The earliest archaeological level so far discovered in the modern city of Waterford dates to the eleventh century. However, an excavation carried out from 2003 to 2007 revealed a Viking settlement 9km west of the present city on the banks of the River Suir at Woodstown. Its discovery has prompted further theories into the foundation and development of Waterford.

It is not clear whether the Woodstown site was a short-lived raiding base or a more permanent settlement. More excavation is required, but so far over 6,000 artefacts have been discovered. Notable findings include balance-weights, a pagan-warrior burial and Kufic dirham (a ninth-century silver Arabic coin). The high amount of broken-up silver (known as hack-silver) suggests that the Vikings used Woodstown as a centre of trade. However, whether they were trading with their Irish neighbours or just with other Vikings still remains unclear.

Woodstown has been dated to the mid to late ninth century, possibly lasting until the beginning of the tenth century. The reason why it was abandoned is unclear, but it could have been because of another settlement downriver at Waterford. The historian Clare Downham believes:

> the present site of Waterford may have been more easily defended … Waterford was closer to the estuaries of the Barrow and Nore … Waterford may have provided a better location for a quay than Woodstown.

There is not yet any archaeological evidence for any habitation at Waterford before the eleventh century, but historians and archaeologists have argued that it is likely there was early settlement around Reginald's Tower and St John's tributary. Earlier histories of the city have placed its foundation at 853, though this seems to be because Gerald of Wales asserts that three brothers, Amalavus, Sitricus and Ivarus, settled in Ireland and correspondingly established the cities of Dublin, Waterford and Limerick. Leaving aside the fact that Gerald was a Norman chronicler writing a couple of centuries later, the tale seems to be a neat foundation myth and Downham rejects its historical accuracy.

The foundation date of Waterford is placed at 914, when the Viking leader Ragnall arrived. Though he left Waterford for Dublin and then York to become a king on both sides of the Irish Sea, the Irish Annals reveal that there was constant settlement at Waterford after that date.

ALL IN THE NAME:
VEDRAFJORDR, *PORT LÁIRGE* AND *LOCH DÁ CHAECH*

Waterford is the only Irish city to retain its Viking name, which is fitting for Ireland's oldest continuous urban settlement. Waterford is older than most northern European capital cities (bar London and Paris). Furthermore, Waterford was Ireland's second city after Dublin until the end of the seventeenth century.

Waterford was known to the Vikings as *Veðrafjǫrðr*, which is believed to mean the Fjord of Castrated Rams, or Windy Fjord. The latter meaning is related to the modern explanation of 'Winter Haven' and would tie in to the possibility that Waterford originated as a winter camp for the raiding Vikings who did not want to risk the stormy sea journey home.

The Irish name for Waterford, *Port Láirge*, means 'Port of a Thigh' with one explanation of the name coming from the *Táin Bó Cúailnge* (a tale from Irish mythology known as the Cattle Raid of Cooley) which tells of how the Brown Bull overcame his foe Findbennach, whose thigh-bone was thrown to *Port Láirge*. One more account comes from the pre-eleventh-century book *Dindshenchas Érenn* which details a young prince called Rot who dies at sea, torn apart by sirens, with his thigh-bone washed ashore at *Port Láirge*. From 915 to 918, the alternative name *Loch dá Chaech* was used for the Waterford harbour area, which translates as 'the lake of the two-blind people'. However, the reason for this remains unclear.

In addition to the origin story told by Gerald of Wales, there is another one in the thirteenth-century biography of the Welsh king, Gruffudd ap Cynan. It claims that the Norwegian king, Harald Finehair, created Dublin and gave

Waterford to his brother, whose descendants continued to rule the city. This era of Waterford's history remains murky, but further archaeological excavation could provide more answers to this fascinating period.

VEDRAFJORDR:
VIKING RULERS TO ANGLO-NORMAN CONQUERORS

Veðrafjǫrðr was a triangular-shaped settlement formed on a tidal inlet at the confluence of the Suir and St John's rivers. It was defended by a fort named Dundory (deemed to have been where Reginald's Tower stands today). Unfortunately, this did not stop the city being destroyed four times in 1031, 1037, 1088 and 1111. This Viking area had three main thoroughfares with High Street being the commercial hub of the city, while four smaller streets intersected the larger streets. Archaeological excavations in the 1980s and '90s uncovered the remains of seventy-two sub-rectangular houses dating from the eleventh and twelfth centuries. These dwellings were constructed with wattle-and-daub walls and thatched roofs. A timber floor of a Viking Age ship was discovered in 1996 by archaeologist Orla Scully whilst excavating a quay wall on the Mall beside the present location of City Hall. The inhabitants of Waterford in the eleventh century were Hiberno-Norse, descendants of the Vikings who had intermarried with the indigenous Irish.

The advancement of the Uí Briain (O'Brien) family to power in Munster led to them ruling Waterford from 976. In 984, the city was the location for the meeting of the King of Munster Brian Boru (and later High King of Ireland) and the sons of Aralt, the Norse King of Limerick. Boru wanted a fleet from Limerick to assist his assault on Dublin, eventually taking place in 1014 at Clontarf. He received support from the Hiberno-Norse of Limerick and Waterford. Though Brian Boru died in battle, the Waterford group overpowered one of his rivals to the high kingship in Máel Sechnail. This defeat leads the historian Eamonn McEneaney to highlight 'the importance of the port towns in Irish politics and the close relationship existing between the native population and the descendants of the original Viking settlers'. These towns had political significance, conferring wealth and status to the rulers who governed them.

The Marriage of Strongbow & Aoife by artist Daniel Maclise was painted in 1854 as an interpretation of a key moment in Irish history, which sees the narratives of Britain and Ireland entwined for centuries (photographic reproduction). *National Gallery of Ireland*

Waterford was starting to transfer allegiance from the kingdom of Munster to Leinster by the eleventh century. In 1037, the city was seized by Diarmait mac Máel na mBó, King of Uí Cheinnselaig (Kinsella); subsequently coins were minted in Waterford under his patronage.

Upon the death of mac Máel na mBó in 1072, Toirdelbach, the grandson of Brian Boru, took control of Leinster and realigned Waterford with Munster after assuming control of the city. He was later succeeded by his son Muirchertach in 1086, who became the most dominant king of Ireland, reigning as High King from 1093 to 1114. In 1088, Waterford was attacked in vain by a rival to the King of Leinster. Diarmait, brother of Muirchertach, was appointed ruler of Waterford in 1096. That same year, the Ostmen (people of mixed Gaelic and Norse ancestry and culture) of Waterford wanted a bishop to lead those who worshipped at buildings such as St Olaf's. This led to Malchus being appointed the first bishop of Waterford that year. He managed to bring Christian practices in line with those of mainland Europe during his forty years in the position.

It is not apparent who succeeded Diarmait, who had deposed his brother in 1114 and died four years later. By 1137, Waterford was protected by King Cormac Mac Cárthaigh (McCarthy) of Desmond when confronted by the forces of Diarmait Mac Murchada of Leinster and Conchobar Ua Briain of Thomond. The western defences of Waterford had been strengthened with a stone wall replacing the timber palisade around the time of the attack.

The city remained under Mac Cárthaigh rule until 1170, when it was besieged by Raymond le Gros and the Anglo-Normans. In aiding the King of Leinster, Diarmait Mac Murchada, to regain his lost kingdom, the marcher lord Richard de Clare, better known as Strongbow, was promised the hand of Aoife, the king's daughter, in marriage. The wedding took place at Christ Church in Waterford, heralding the end of the Viking Age in Ireland. Upon the death of the King of Leinster the following year, Henry II, King of England reached Waterford where he received the submission of Diarmait Mac Cárthaigh.

The Anglo-Norman invasion not only signaled the end of the Viking Age in Ireland but, with the marriage of Strongbow and Aoife, entwined the histories of Britain and Ireland for the centuries that follow.

Additionally, the Anglo-Normans altered the make-up of Irish towns with new defences, as well as introducing new customs and traits. The importance of the ceremony which took place in Christ Church is depicted in Daniel Maclise's *The Marriage of Strongbow and Aoife*, painted in 1854. The oil painting was to be hung at the House of Lords in Westminster to mark the colonisation of the British Empire. The scene shows dead Irish warriors and a broken Celtic harp, while Strongbow stands on a damaged high cross as the old ways are destroyed by the Norman conquerors.

Eamonn McEneaney believes of the defeat of the Vikings in Ireland by the Anglo-Normans that:

> It is ironic that the Vikings, founders of Ireland's first towns, with their expertise in naval matters and improved weapons technology, should turn out to act as catalyst for the development of a more centralised Ireland, making it possible for the Anglo-Normans to achieve a foothold over a major part of the island in the decades after 1170.

TURGESIUS: NINTH-CENTURY VIKING RAIDER

Turgesius, after whom a tower which defended the city of Waterford was named, was a ninth-century Viking raider. Though historians are dubious of Turgesius existing, his Norse name was Thorgestr, with the Irish being Turgéis. He reached Dublin Bay with a large fleet in 837 and when he came to the mouth of the River Boyne took command of all Irish Vikings. The river system of Ireland allowed him to penetrate deeply into the island. Turgesius lay waste to Armagh in 841 and according to unreliable sources, possibly desecrated the altar of Clonmacnoise by making love to his wife Ota there in 844. He then declared her high priestess. The Viking invader drowned in Lough Owel in County Westmeath in 845.

KITE BROOCH:
'FINEST EXAMPLE OF VIKING-AGE METALWORK'

The Kite Brooch, weighing 20.6g, was crafted around 1090 and is considered one of the best examples of personal jewellery from the Viking Age, made from silver and adorned with gold foil and amethyst glass studs.

It was discovered by archaeologists during the excavations that coincided with the construction of the City Square Shopping Centre in Waterford City. Brooches were decorations on metal pins which would have been used to fasten a cloak and such implements were used until the early fourteenth century when buttons came into fashion.

Such an elaborate brooch would have been worn by those of high status (men or women); only thirteen kite brooches survive in Ireland. Made of gold and silver, the Waterford Kite Brooch resembled a charcoal-like object when found by archaeologists, as silver attracts impurities.

The Waterford Kite Brooch is one of the most impressive examples of secular metalwork of the late eleventh and early twelfth centuries. It reflects indigenous Irish traditions with Scandinavian influences due to Waterford's strong connections with the Vikings. *Courtesy of Waterford Treasures*

After months of conservation, the true beauty of the object became apparent and can now be clearly seen on display in Reginald's Tower.

It is a fusion of Irish, English, Scandinavian and continental European designs. The Hiberno-Norse elements are indicative of Waterford in the twelfth century. The body of the brooch is a cast hollow silver kite-shaped box which would have been attached to a hinge and long pin to fasten the cloak. It appears that the goldsmith would have used a numerical plan by which to design the brooch. The length of the pin would have been longer than what is currently attached to the brooch. Even the length of pin would have been an indicator of a person's status.

The Kite Brooch is a demonstration of the craftsmanship of those who inhabited Waterford around this time.

BUILDINGS WITH EARLY MEDIEVAL ORIGINS

Christ Church Cathedral:
One of the Most Historic Sites in Ireland

In 1096, Waterford was granted its first bishop, though it is considered that the city's first cathedral was not constructed until after 1152. The original cathedral predates the Anglo-Norman invasion of 1170 but was later refurbished in 1210. Christ Church Cathedral is where the marriage ceremony of Strongbow and Aoife took place. The significance of this event is that the histories of both Britain and Ireland were entwined for the next 800 years. The Anglo-Normans built a Gothic cathedral in the thirteenth century which was replaced by the present Christ Church Cathedral in the eighteenth century.

The Medieval cathedral had a central nave and chancel with aisles on either side, with a tower on one side. Over subsequent centuries, chapels were added. The archaeologist Dave Pollock reports that '[t]he floor level of the old cathedral is well below the present granite slabs. A decorated pier of the medieval building can be seen, standing on a mortar floor 1.8m down. The plain finish on the old floor may overlie paving or tiles.'

The current cathedral was designed by local architect John Roberts in the 1770s and contains parts of the old church from the early thirteenth century, such as the remains of an Anglo-Norman cluster of pillars. Legend has it that Bishop Chenevix was disinclined for the new cathedral to be built in a Georgian style, so it is believed that a ruse was devised to change his mind. Prospective builders organised that rubble would fall along the bishop's path as he walked through the cathedral. After this, Chenevix believed that a new cathedral was essential. During the demolition, gunpowder was used to knock down the medieval cathedral.

Primarily made from limestone, the neo-Classical cathedral was finished in 1779, costing £5,397. Christ Church Cathedral encompasses an eight-bay double-height nave with a single-bay four-staged tower close towards the entrance. The original interior has changed from the eighteenth century due to a fire in the organ gallery in 1815. It was remodelled in 1891 by Sir Thomas Drew. This led to the ground floor windows being blocked out and the removal of square pews and galleries. There was also a construction of a new case for the organ.

The organ was restored in 2003 and moved to a new gallery in its original location. Commissioned in 1817, the Elliot organ was placed in the corner of Christ Church Cathedral post the late nineteenth-century refashioning of the church. The organ has a solid mahogany case encompassing gold-plated pipes. It is deemed one of the best organs on the island outside of Dublin. The cathedral also houses the gothic cadaver tomb of James Rice, Mayor of Waterford on eleven occasions during the fifteenth century. The tomb (which Rice shares with his wife Katherine Broun) was in a chapel built by Rice connected to the original Anglo-Norman cathedral. It has been moved twice in the Georgian cathedral and has been placed at its present location since 1880. The message of the tomb is illustrated by its Latin inscription which translates: 'I am what you will be; I was what you are now.'

Reginald's Tower:
Ireland's Oldest Urban Civic Building

Reginald's tower – a massive hinge of stone connecting the two great outspread wings, the Quay and the Mall, within which lay the body of the city.

Thomas Francis Meagher, *Recollections of Waterford* (Easter Week 1843)

Reginald's Tower and the Quay, Waterford, *c.* 1890 to *c.* 1900. *Library of Congress*

Ireland's oldest urban civic building, Reginald's Tower, appears to be named after the tenth-century Viking ruler of Waterford, Ragnall, or one of his successors bearing the same name. It seems that the Vikings had a fortification at this location from the tenth century. The tower was built to defend the entrance to Waterford, and the present structure was built in two stages. The ground and first floor were completed in the late twelfth century while the upper floors were constructed in the fifteenth century to accommodate the use of cannon.

The original access point to the tower is at the second storey, with there now being two entry points at ground-floor level. One of these later doorways (inserted into the tower in the 1590s) led to a sixteenth-century blockhouse where cannons were kept. The blockhouse was demolished in 1714. A cannonball is lodged in the top of the tower, dating from the siege of Waterford by the forces of Oliver Cromwell in 1650.

Waterford City – A History

Above left: Reginald's Tower and Poole's Studios around 1910. A.H. Poole operated as a commercial photographer in the city from 1884 to 1954. His collection is housed in the National Library of Ireland and provides a fascinating insight into the social and economic state of Waterford of the period. *Poole Collection WP0363, National Library of Ireland*

Above right: Reginald's Tower in the twenty-first century.

Inside the tower, the stumble steps or spiral stairs are built into the walls of the structure. These steps are intentionally set at different elevations to make them problematic for would-be aggressors to ascend. The fifty-six steps are angled to the right to make it hard for right-handed attackers to swing their swords. The walls at ground-floor level are almost 4m in thickness.

In the subsequent centuries, Reginald's Tower has been used as a prison, a mint and a defensive fortification. It served as a prison from 1819 to 1850, mainly to detain petty criminals and drunks. The last prisoner to be held in the tower was Meg Collender, who was sentenced to two weeks' imprisonment for drunk and disorderly behaviour. She had been a repeat offender, having committed the same offence 150 times. While a prison, the top floor of the tower became known as the 'ballroom', as it was where the female prisoners were kept and would pass the time by singing and dancing.

The tower subsequently became the official residence of the High Constable of Waterford, the last of whom was James O'Mahony who died in Reginald's Tower in 1901. Today, the tower is a museum which houses artefacts related to Viking Waterford and the Woodstown excavations. It is managed by the Office of Public Works.

The Dearg-doo:
the Waterford Vampire and the First Frog to be Seen in Ireland

An unusual tale has been linked to Reginald's Tower, although the link remains tenuous. The English clergyman Montague Summers noted in his quirky studies on vampires and werewolves that in 'ancient Ireland the Vampire was generally known as *Dearg-dul*, "red blood sucker" with numerous attempts of Anglicisation and corruption of the Gaelic name leading to the terms *Dearg-doo* or *Dearg-due* being most commonly used'. Summers continues:

> At Waterford, in Ireland, there is a little graveyard under a ruined church near Strongbow's Tower. Legend has it that underneath the ground at this spot there lies a beautiful female vampire still ready to kill those she can lure thither by her beauty.

Some believe the vampire is the spirit of Strongbow himself, while others suggest it is that of his wife Aoife. Perhaps the idea of a female vampire being that of Aoife comes from the rather grisly story of her death. As a young woman, upon the death of her husband in 1176 she had a fortress constructed at Cappamore to protect her territory and raise her children while feuding with the Quinn family. However, she died by an arrow through her throat, fired by the Quinns, and was subsequently interred in a crypt in Kilkenny Castle.

The Vampire (1897) by Philip Burne-Jones. The tale of the Dearg-doo, the Waterford Vampire, is an interesting story that grew over the centuries, with its possible origins being that of the first frog to be seen in Ireland being in Waterford.

Of the myth of the Waterford vampire, Summers notes:

> No authority is given for this, which is perhaps hardly surprising when one knows that there is not nor ever was such a tower at Waterford as 'Strongbow's Tower'. Probably there is some confused reference to 'Reginald's Tower', which Strongbow (de Clare, Earl of Pembroke) used as a fortress in 1170, and where King John established a mint, whence it was called Dundory. The great Irish authority, the late Chevalier W.H. Gratton-Flood informed me that there is no legend of a Vampire connected with Reginald's Tower, and probably the following tale has been confused which is related in regard to the capture of Waterford by the Anglo-Normans by Giraldus Cambrensis in his Topographia Hibernica. A frog was found in the grassy meadows near Waterford, and was brought alive to Cork before Robert le Poer, the warden of the city (who lived in Reginald's Tower). All were astonished at the sight of the frog, this being the first frog discovered in Ireland. It is said that the frog was solemnly interred in Reginald's Tower. Cambrensis notes that the frog must have been brought over by Strongbow among the baggage of the force he led from England.

Giraldus Cambrensis, also known as Gerald of Wales, was a Cambro-Norman archdeacon of Breton and historian, a cousin of the Anglo-Norman lords. He came with them to Ireland and recorded their actions in *The Conquest of Ireland*. The tale of the frog comes from his Topography, which describes the land of Ireland. The Topography displays many prejudices towards the native Irish, portraying them as barbaric savages.

A HISTORY OF ALCOHOL IN WATERFORD
from the Earliest Times to the Nineteenth Century

I was a day in Waterford,
There was wine and punch on the table,
There was the full of the house of women there,
And myself drinking their health.

Portlairge (Translation of Traditional Irish Song)

Prior to the arrival of monks from the continent in the twelfth century, alcohol would have been seasonally consumed, while the holy men brought a thirst and understanding for distilled liquors and wine.

The monasteries limited the use of distilled liquors for medicinal purposes, which is reflected in the name it was known by up until the eighteenth century, *aqua vitae*. While the Irish term *uisce beatha* (fire water) was in use by the sixteenth century, it would appear to spread after the dissolution of the monasteries in 1540, with it being noted its effects 'sets the Irish amadinge and breeds much mischieve' from 1584. Such developments can be seen with the use of words such as *poitin* and *builechin* meaning 'a blow in the head'.

The advent of the Normans in Ireland brought an increased demand for such alcohol, which formed part of the dispute between the neighbouring ports of New Ross and Waterford over which had the right to import wine (for more on the trade dispute between Waterford and the neighbouring port of New Ross, see page 52). Wine was popular among all ages as it was better to drink than the contaminated water of the city. Waterford was the medieval wine capital of Ireland, as records show that more wine was imported through the port of the city than any other of the island. From the wine trade, Waterford was connected to European cities such as Bordeaux, Bristol and Bruges. The cross-pollination of trade and culture can be seen with the French merchant Eymar de Godar of Gascony settling in Waterford. He served as the Mayor of Waterford on four occasions between 1304 and 1313.

Medieval wine barrels. Waterford was the medieval wine capital of Ireland due to its extensive trading links. It would form part of one of the longest-running legal disputes in Europe, between Waterford and the neighbouring port of New Ross.

In relation to the consumption of beer, there is no Irish word for that type of alcohol, which would lead one to believe that it was a later arrival to Ireland. The advantage of the beer being transportable via barrels and not going off would aid its popularity in Ireland. The Mayor of Waterford, Richard Cromwell, decreed in 1658:

> it is found by dayly experiences that many mischieves and inconveniences do arise from the excessive number of alehouses, from the erection of them in woods, bogs and other unfit places. And many of them not in townships but dispersed by and in dangerous places and kept by unknown persons not undertaken for, whereby many times they become receptacles for rebels and other malefactors, and harbours for gamesters and other idle, disordered and unprofitable livers …

From this decree, each alehouse was to require a licence and that they needed to be located within towns and villages while also providing suitable accommodation for travellers. The historian Des Cowman wrote 'it is likely that such alcohol as was made for popular consumption in the 17th century was beer'.

By the middle of the seventeenth century in Waterford City, there were four malt houses located along Barronstrand Street and John Street. It seems that the malt was for home use rather than supplied to breweries as there was only one brewery at this time, a shed 19ft by 12ft in size behind a house at Milk Lane.

A new malt house was established outside the confines of the city walls on 'Bricken's Green' by 1669, while an increase in brewing led the corporation to warn about fire hazards by cautioning to 'all common brewers and others, from lodging great quantities of furze in cellars and other parts of their house'. The use of furze as an additive to alcohol may have been for taste.

The commercialisation of alcohol develops around the start of the eighteenth century, as the poorer classes imbibed beer rather than quenching their thirst with dirty water. Such beer was either made at home, known as 'table beer', or could be bought on the street from jug-carrying women. Wine was the indulgence of the wealthy, as beverages such as tea and coffee were not commonly obtainable at the time.

The year 1770 saw 200 gallons of beer imported from England to Waterford every month. Throughout the 1770s and '80s, newspapers were filled with advertisements for ales and beers. By 1786, the importation of beer to Waterford had doubled since 1770 as the use of hops in local brewing decreased by 20 per cent over the same timeframe. Irish brewers had a tax disadvantage compared with their English counterparts (which favoured beer over whiskey) and thus fell behind in the process.

A commission recording the number of brewers in Ireland noted that in Waterford in 1790 there were seven strong brewers (specialising in new kinds of beer with hops and sugar) and three small brewers (manufacturing traditional 'table beer'), but the report stated that there were zero retailers of alcohol brewing their own drink in the city. However, 1792 saw the *Waterford Herald* report that 'William Strangman and Company inform their friends and the public that they have begun the strong ale and beer brewing'.

By the early nineteenth century, there were at least nine breweries operating in Waterford over different periods, with three surviving to the 1840s. The obvious growth in breweries in the city was partially due to new incentives for brewing introduced by the government. These breweries were as follows:

Strangman and Davis, brewing from 1792, with it believed that Strangman, a local merchant, provided the capital for the venture, and Davis likely offered the site of the enterprise at Mary Street.

Grant and Barron, location unknown, advertisement in the *Waterford Mirror* in 1802.

Joseph Dwyer at Rose Lane (promoting English cider for sale).

Carroll and McGrath's, again location unknown but was advertised for sale in 1806.

Hearn's, located at Johnsbridge, suffered a substantial fire in 1810 and was sold the following year to *Hunt, Leonard and Co.*, which sought to sell the enterprise in 1820 leading to apparent closure.

Birnie and Lynhams situated on the corner of Stephen's Street and New Street; it is believed to have been in existence from 1800 and

The Cooperage Department of Henry Downes at 10 Thomas Street, 31 October 1936. *National Library of Ireland*

The cellar of H. Downes & Co., October 1936. The bar is still in existence and blends and bottles its popular No. 9 Irish whiskey, which it has for over two centuries. *National Library of Ireland*

entered new ownership in the 1830s under Dunford and Condon before being given over to William Kiely, who possessed it until the end of the nineteenth century.

Cherry's had breweries established at Peter Street and O'Connell Street before 1802; the Peter Street operation was closed, with production eventually being concentrated by 1870 at their New Ross brewery (which opened in 1835); in 1955, *Cherry's* returned to Waterford when taking over Strangman's brewery on Mary Street but then formed part of the Guinness group.

Robinson and O'Brien's started at Newgate Street in 1812 and moved to Barrack Street by 1817; Robinson left the partnership with the enterprise being known as *O'Brien and Sons*, which ceased trading in 1839.

Barronstrand Street Brewery was a brief venture in the 1830s, with an output of fifty barrels a week, and was placed for sale in 1839.

Ryland recorded in his *History, Topography and Antiquities … of Waterford* that by 1824 'the brewers of Waterford have brought the manufacture of beer and porter to such perfection as to supercede the necessity of importation from England'. Five thousand barrels of beer had been imported from England to Waterford in 1786 and that was reduced to just two in 1824. The increase in beer brewing led to Waterford exporting to England, but was to the detriment of distillers in the city: the closures of *Dobbs and Hobbs* (after 1801), William Grant at Alexander Lane (placed for sale in 1807) and *Ramsey and Bell's* was placed for sale in 1814. Although whiskey blenders continued to sate the thirsty of the city, rum began to rival whiskey in Waterford.

By the 1840s, Waterford had reached its highpoint in brewing, which would be altered by the creation of the Temperance Movement by Father Matthew and the development of the railways in the latter half of the nineteenth century, which aided the domination of Guinness in the Irish market, as Waterford brewers who adapted and competed with their English opponents struggled by the end of the 1880s.

2

A ROYAL CITY:
Anglo-Norman Waterford

TIMELINE

1170 CE: Noted in the *Annals of the Four Masters,* Richard de Clare or Strongbow imprisons the Lord of the Deisi, Ua Faelain and his son and kills 700 prisoners.

1171 CE: On 17 October, Henry II lands at Crooke, Passage East, with an expeditionary force of 240 ships carrying 4,000 soldiers. He arrived at Waterford the following day, the first time an English King had entered an Irish city.

1173 CE: At a synod of bishops taking place at Christ Church Cathedral in Waterford, the Papal Bull *Laudabiliter* is read publicly for the first time in Ireland, fifteen years after it was first pronounced. The bull decreed that Ireland was under the control of the English King.

1185 CE: Prince John arrives in Waterford; while there, he endows the Benedictine Priory of St John the Evangelist.

1204 CE: King John establishes a mint in Waterford and permits its inhabitants to hold an annual eight-day fair.

1215 CE: King John grants Waterford a charter, just a few short weeks after issuing Magna Carta.

1226 CE: The Friary of St Saviours is established for the Dominican Friars after being granted by King Henry III, and becomes known as Blackfriars.

1228 CE: On 16 July, Henry III petitions Pope Gregory IX to unify the Sees of Waterford and Lismore. It takes 135 years before the dioceses are united.

1240 CE: Sir Hugh Purcell founds the Franciscan Friary.

1252 CE: Waterford is destroyed by fire.

1274 CE: King Edward I grants the citizens of Waterford the right to elect a mayor.

1284 CE: Roger le Lom is the first name documented as the Mayor of Waterford.

1345 CE: The Powers lay waste to the land surrounding Waterford City.

1349 CE: The Bubonic Plague causes devastation to the city. The Black Death wipes out around a third of its population.

1363 CE: Pope Urban V unites the dioceses of Waterford and Lismore with Thomas le Reve as bishop.

WATERFORD:
from Viking Settlement to Royal City

The economic and political fortunes of the city of Waterford began to flourish from the arrival of the Anglo-Normans in 1170, capitalising on its geographic proximity to ports such as Bristol, which was one of the most significant ports in medieval England. King Henry II of England made Waterford a royal city, thus creating the foundations in which the city would begin to govern itself and its commercial affairs. Upon landing at Waterford, Henry II became the first English monarch to set foot on the island of Ireland.

The Ostmen were expelled from the confines of the original Viking settlement of the city and relocated to an area outside the city now known as Ballybricken. This 'Ostmantown' later formed part of the Anglo-Norman extension of Waterford as the city grew organically. In addition, the quays of the city were extended as new merchants and traders wanted to preserve control of the port.

Kings of the medieval period granted charters to favoured areas, giving them special privileges under the feudal system. They allowed wealthy merchant families to control the internal activities of the city, with trade being a priority. Charters conferred upon Waterford include that of 1215 by King John which saw elected representatives of Waterford's merchant class obtain control of the courts. Previously, John had allowed the city to stage an annual eight-day fair in August to entice foreign traders to do business with Waterford. He inaugurated a mint at Reginald's Tower around 1195–96 which closed in 1204 but was re-established in 1210.

The English king strengthened the defences of the city with three new stone gates erected prior to 1212, named Arundell Gate, Colbeck Gate and St Martin's Gate. In addition, Reginald's Tower was reconstructed as the city expanded westwards with the creation of Barronstrand Street and John Street. Over this period Waterford adopted the narrow-styled streets and laneways typical of the medieval era. Such streets had to connect to the gateways of Waterford. Ballybricken was linked with the forming of Patrick Street, as those travelling from the north of the city would have to cross the River Suir and enter Waterford via Ballybricken. To the south of the city, John's Hill and Johnstown were developed, as travellers entered Waterford by crossing John's Bridge. Broad Street became the focal point of the commercial activities of the city and Michael Street and Stephen Street date from the thirteenth and fourteenth centuries as Waterford continued to expand under the Anglo-Normans. The Anglo-Norman extension appeared to act as a separate entity from the original Viking triangle, with the city walls bolstering the sense of difference between the two areas of Waterford.

King John of England from Cassell's *History of England* published in 1902. John granted a charter in 1215 to Waterford, which can be viewed as the 'birth certificate' of the city.

THE MAYORALTY OF WATERFORD CITY:
One of the Oldest Civic Institutions in Europe

In 1272, Waterford was given the right to elect a mayor. Previously, the city had to pay a fixed sum of 100 marks to the king, which was the second highest rent paid by an Irish city. The mayor was held personally responsible for the debts of the city, which had to be accounted for each year to the Exchequer. Waterford's superior claim to all foreign ships docking at its harbour, to the detriment of neighbouring New Ross, was sustained by successive English monarchs, maintaining a period of prosperity for the city. It was also designated a wine port, and in 1232 King Henry III of England conferred the right to pay half the tax paid by other Irish ports, thus making Waterford the medieval wine capital of Ireland.

A mint was re-established in Waterford in 1281 with Roger de Lom as its keeper. It subsequently closed the following year but reopened twelve years later under the auspices of Roger the Goldsmith. A lot of this wealth came from the city's substantial interest in the wool and hide trade. King Edward I introduced the Great New Custom to fund his campaign against the Scots, with Waterford generating around one-fifth of the total of the tax take for the Anglo-Norman colony.

MEDIEVAL DEVOTION IN WATERFORD:
Disease, Death and Commerce

The Middle Ages also saw many churches and monasteries established in Waterford. King John permitted the citizens to develop Christ Church Cathedral in the Gothic style, with construction beginning in 1210. The Dominican and Franciscan orders' arrival in the city saw Waterford embrace the religious movements developing across Europe. The Franciscans built their friary around 1240, aided by the finance of Sir Hugh Purcell, and it was known as Greyfriars as the friars wore habits made from grey cloth.

Such devotional practices are reflected in the naming of streets within the original Viking settlement. Peter's Street, Lady Lane and Olaf's Street are all named after churches, while the Anglo-Norman streets such as John, Michael and Stephen are also called so after places of worship and religious practice.

The city's fortunes changed in 1349 when the Black Death arrived in Ireland, wiping out nearly one-third of Waterford's 3,000 population. This led to a decline in local trade as merchants sought to develop ties with other European ports. In addition, the city did not expand past the thirteenth-century city walls due to the bubonic plague.

The city continued trying to prosper despite adverse circumstances. In the 1370s, one of Waterford's most remarkable artefacts was created. The Great Charter Roll is one of the most unusual documents from the period and was used in the long-running trade dispute with the neighbouring port of New Ross. Waterford was trying to preserve its status as an influential port city, with royal benefits that New Ross did not have. In order to convince Edward III that they had a better claim than New Ross, they sewed all the royal charters given to Waterford into a 4m-long charter roll. It was illustrated with the images of several English kings to visually demonstrate the city's longstanding loyalty to the crown. It was a last-ditch attempt to extend the golden age of Waterford.

CITY WALLS:
Largest Collection of Medieval Urban Defences in Ireland

The earliest reference to the defences of Waterford is in 1088 in the *Annals of Ireland*. There is an indication of the Hiberno-Norse fortifications of the city by Gerald of Wales when Waterford was seized by the Anglo-Normans in 1170. One such invader, Raymond le Gros, observed that 'a small building overhanging the city wall supported on the outside by a beam' collapsed when attacked, taking a large portion of the city wall with it. This aided the defeat of the Hiberno-Norse by the Anglo-Normans. A substantial building programme was undertaken to improve and strengthen the defences of Waterford in the following decades.

As the city expanded westwards, at least three new gates were erected to facilitate the defence of Waterford during the reign of King John (built prior to 1212). By the end of the Medieval era, Waterford was enclosed by stone walls with numerous towers along it. The wall which ran along the Quay was demolished by the early eighteenth century, though the remains of eight of the original thirty towers can be seen today:

> The Beach Tower located at Jenkin's Lane is one of the most impressive towers of the medieval defences, with fifteenth-century Irish crenellations.

> The Double Tower situated near the end of Castle Street contains two interior chambers, hence its name. There is a passageway from one of the chambers to the Benedictine priory of St John which is close by to the tower.

> The French Tower is at the top of Castle Street adjacent to Brown's Lane.

> Reginald's Tower is Ireland's oldest urban civic building positioned at the apex of the Viking Triangle.

> St Martin's Gate was one of three defensive stations of the original Viking settlement and can be found at Spring Garden Alley.

> A semi-lunar tower can be found behind De La Salle on Patrick Street.

> Turgesius' Tower is named after a Viking chief from the ninth century. The base of the tower was found in 2009 during the redevelopment of Penney's department store.

> The Watch Tower is a cylindrically shaped tower located at Manor Street and dates to the thirteenth century.

One of the last defensive structures of the city's defences to be demolished was Colbeck Gate in the early eighteenth century. Located at the junction of Colbeck Street and the Mall, it was also known as the 'chamber of green cloth'. The earliest reference to the gate comes from an inquisition of 1224 which refers to St Katherine's Gate, which may have been another name for

Left: The Beach Tower, Jenkin's Lane. *Centre:* The French Tower. *Right:* The Watch Tower.

the landmark. Over the course of the seventeenth century, Colbeck Gate was used as a prison, a private dwelling and as an arms store. The year 1680 saw an order that 'ammunition belonging to the city [was] to be lodged in the garret of Colbeck Castle'.

KING JOHN AND 'THE BIRTH CERTIFICATE' OF WATERFORD CITY

King John was the ruler of England and Ireland together from 1199 to 1216, with the Magna Carta being the apex of his legacy. In relation to Waterford, John's Charter of Incorporation, granted to the city in 1215, is of great significance. The historian Eamonn McEneaney writes that the 1215 charter 'is the Birth Certificate of the city'. The English monarch took a personal interest in the welfare of the inhabitants of the city, even visiting Waterford twice, firstly in 1185 as Lord of Ireland and returning in 1210 bearing the same title and that of King of England.

John was made Lord of Ireland in 1177 by his father Henry II, perhaps visualising Ireland as a distinct kingdom to be ruled by his descendants. John's first visit to the city took place on 25 April 1185, accompanied by Giraldus Cambrensis, who noted that the prince had failed to make the customary visit to St David's Shrine when leaving Wales, which appeared to be a rather ominous sign for the visit ahead. Waterford was the second most significant city during John's lordship of Ireland.

A Royal City: Anglo-Norman Waterford

In Waterford, the *Irish of the Decies* came to pay homage to John but were treated rudely by the prince's Norman entourage who mocked their style of dress and even pulled at the beards of the Irish. Prince of the Decies, Melaghlin O Faelain left Waterford straightaway after receiving this reception and proceeded to tell the other Irish princes of their treatment by King Henry II's son. The Irish prince commented: 'The King's son, [is] a mere stripling, surrounded and counselled by striplings like himself.'

During the trip John embarked on building three castles at Ardfinnan, Lismore and Tibberaghny to protect the area of the Decies and to create a foothold which would allow him to progress further into Munster. His aim was to strengthen and expand the Norman authority in Ireland.

John returned to the city in 1210, having become King of England in 1199 upon the death of his brother Richard I. The year he was crowned, John made grants to the Priory of St John near the city such as allowing the Benedictine monks to trade without having to pay any taxes. Five years later, he granted Waterford the right to stage a fair every August to encourage trade.

His second visit to the city was to restrain the Norman plutocrats who were conducting themselves freely of his rule. Landing at Crooke, John's visit to Waterford is believed to have prompted the building of the city walls. This process of fortification was to protect the city from external forces. In the accounts of the Sheriff of County Waterford it is recorded in 1212 that the inhabitants owed £144 5s 8d for the development.

The Charter of Incorporation granted by John in 1215 established the city as a distinct body from the county. It allowed the citizens of the city to administer justice within its confines as well as establishing that all vessels entering Waterford Harbour had to unload at Waterford, though some academics believe this charter to be a forgery.

The king had an interest in urban development, which can be seen with him granting charters to Liverpool in 1206 and Dublin in 1215. The issuing of such charters was for the monarch to maintain the loyalty of his dominions, which was particularly important with Waterford as it was the first port of call for any royal visit to Ireland. The charter to Waterford was issued on 3 July 1215. This would form part of the issues related to the city's trade dispute with the neighbouring port of New Ross. This was compounded further as the charter was never enrolled in 1215 in the Charter Rolls of King John, possibly due to objections from William Marshal, the second Earl of Pembroke, who sought to promote the interests of New Ross.

Further controversy related to the charter of King John occurred when, in 1603, the Lord Deputy of Ireland and his army were not permitted entry to Waterford by the city's mayor. The mayor claimed that the charter of 1215 allowed him to refuse entrance to the city. The Lord Deputy had proceeded to Waterford to proclaim the accession to the throne by James I upon the death of Queen Elizabeth I. He was eventually granted admittance to the city after threatening to cut down the charter in question with his sword.

The first official reference to King John's charter to the city comes in 1618, when James I granted the city a charter which confirmed all previous charters that had been endowed to Waterford.

THE LEPER HOSPITAL:
from Sickness in the Middle Ages to the Infirmary

Leprosy was one of the most contagious diseases in the Middle Ages, and led to sufferers of the illness being segregated from society.

Ryland notes that King John was the founder of the Leper Hospital in 1211 (at the area now made up of New Street and Stephen's Street) in thanks for his two sons being cured of a skin disease which mirrored leprosy, though Charles Smith records that the hospital was founded by the Powers of Dunhill (though it is likely that the Powers provided the first grant which was enhanced by the English king's gift).

However, it is more likely that the Leper Hospital was founded by Robert le Poer (Power) in 1185 and was situated within 800 acres of land for its maintenance. King John gave it another 900 acres on the provision that those who suffered from leprosy prayed for him daily. The majority of this land was near Dunmore East in an area still known as Leperstown to this day. Additional land included the area from John's Bridge to Johnstown, spanning John's Hill to Ballytruckle.

Around the time of the Reformation, the hospital came under the control of the corporation. By the middle of the seventeenth century, the Leper Hospital had fallen into a state of ruin. It was decided by Waterford Corporation that the hospital was for the treatment of lepers only. In a tale, a man with a broken leg is said to have responded when told he was not a leper, 'Oh bedad, this is the greatest leper in the country; he has lept into the river and broken his leg.' Perhaps this wry quip earned him a bed in the hospital.

In relation to later cases of leprosy, Richard Lahert records:

> In 1707 the case of a leperess named Margaret Slattery was reported, and that of Richard Francis, 'lame and afflicted with leprosy', in 1713, when he was admitted to the Hospital, then in a very bad state of repair. In 1723, Mary Tobin was ordered to the Leper House by Doctors Reynet and Dougan and, we are told, the last leper in Ireland was an inmate of the institution in 1775, despite the fact that Dr Boates, *c.* 1650, stated that leprosy was then extinct in Ireland for many years.

It is said that the skeleton of the highwayman William Crotty was on display in the hospital as a curiosity. By the 1780s, the corporation sought for a new hospital to be built. The Infirmary was built in 1824 at John's Hill with the founding of the body known as the County and City Infirmary in 1896. The nineteenth-century building could accommodate fifty-four patients with a staff of twenty-five doctors and nurses.

BALLYBRICKEN

No guidebook to Waterford would be complete without a reference to Ballybricken. It is one of the oldest place names in Waterford, as it is one of the most historic in the annals of the city. For generations it was the recognised gathering place for all big meetings. O'Connell held a great Repeal meeting on Ballybricken Hill … All Waterford fairs are held on Ballybricken, and it is the recognised centre of the livestock and bacon-curing industries. In many ways it is as well-known as Waterford itself.

A bustling market scene of Ballybricken from 4 May 1910. The area was a hub for the bacon industry in the city. *Poole Collection WP 2103, National Library of Ireland*

The Humours of Ballybricken

*So now to the end we'll still defend,
The rights that freedom gave us
We all will stand to free our land
From those who would enslave us
When Stuart comes with fifes and drums
And freedom's friend's his seeking
There we'll find one leg behind
In Waterford's Ballybricken.*

Irish Trade Union Congress, Waterford,
August 1939: Souvenir and Guide

The name Ballybricken stems from the Irish *Baile Bhric-Ghein* which was shortened to *Baile Bricín*, translating as the 'town of the tribe of Bric'. The *Uí Bhric* were a faction of the *Deise* which settled in east Munster in the third century after being expelled from the kingdom of Meath as a result of killing the son of the High King. Today the area includes the Green and surrounding streets and laneways.

Ballybricken Green is ancient in its origin. On the seventeenth-century Downs Survey map, Ballybricken was labelled as the 'Great Green'. On entering the city, one could travel through the Green towards St Patrick's Gate. Some travellers could take the ferry at Grannagh and pass through Ballybricken, which the founder of the Methodist faith, John Wesley, did in June 1750.

The area was the location for the citadel or St Patrick's Fort (which is explored later in this book), which became the city prison and now is the site of the city's Garda Headquarters.

The main industry of Ballybricken was that of bacon and livestock. A popular pursuit in the area was bull baiting with the Bull Post, which can still be seen today, a remnant of this blood sport. Former Attorney General of Ireland John Edward Walsh noted in his book *Ireland Sixty Years Ago* (published in 1847) that:

> The south of Ireland, connected by several ties with Spain, adopted many Spanish usages and sports, among the rest, bull fighting, which degenerated into bull baiting … The place for baiting then [in the early eighteenth century] was an open space outside the city gate, called Ballybricken. It was surrounded with houses, from which spectators looked on, as at a Spanish bull fight. In the centre the ring through which the rope was passed. It was surmounted by a pole, bearing a large copper bull on a vane. In 1798, when bull baits were prohibited, this apparatus was removed, and the sport discontinued; But prior to that it was followed with the greatest enthusiasm, and it was not unusual to see eighteen or twenty of these animals baited during the season.

Some sought to remove the Bull Post in the late nineteenth century but Alderman John Redmond rebuked this by saying, 'The Bull Post is one of the landmarks of this City, and you might as well remove Reginald's Tower on the Quay as the venerable but neglected pile. The Bull Post is to

Waterford what the Treaty Stone is to Limerick and the Blarney Stone to Cork.' It now is a popular spot for people to chat and take in the hustle and bustle of the area.

Ballybricken became synonymous with cattle markets, and the earliest known reference to a marketplace in the area was of the Market House in 1680. Some of the surrounding areas benefitted from these markets, primarily in the bacon industry. Bacon factories in Waterford City included:

> Francis E. Barnes, Summerhill, was one of the oldest bacon factories in Ireland located at the top of Bridge Street. Beginning in 1820 under a Mr Milward,, it later came under the control of Francis E. Barnes with the odd position of its cellars allowing them to cure bacon at times of the year in which other competitors couldn't.

> J. Matterson and Sons Limited was started in 1826 in Limerick with a branch established in Waterford at the Glen in 1873. The products of Matterson were popular in the English market and such was the demand that it led to 250 people working in the Waterford factory.

> Henry Denny and Sons was established around the 1820s and operated in the city until the 1970s. Denny and his method of bacon curing are detailed in the chapter on the nineteenth century in the city.

> Queen's Bacon Factory progressed from its Mary Street premises established around 1840 to a 10-acre site at Morgan Street. Employing up to 150 workers, the factory killed nearly 3,500 animals per week.

On 28 July 1809, a great fire took place destroying nearly sixty houses in less than an hour. It is believed that the fire was an accident and that dry weather had compounded the damage. There was a single fatality with the death, that of a 4-year-old boy.

A church was built at Ballybricken during the pastorate of Fr Pierce Power (1807–28) and named the Church of the Holy Trinity (Without), as it was situated outside the city walls of Waterford City. It replaced a thatched

Faha chapel which was situated in what are now the grounds of Mount Sion. By 1836, a steeple and bell tower were added to the church under the stewardship of Fr Michael Fitzgerald.

THE DEVELOPMENT OF BALLYBRICKEN INTO A HUB OF THE PIG AND BACON INDUSTRY

A pig market was held twice weekly from 1831, while monthly fairs made the locale bustling with commercial interests. The change in selling livestock through the mart system in the 1950s saw the last fair to be held on the Green in 1955. A cattle mart was built on Ballybricken Green and continued until 1977 (with a mart developed on the old Kilmeadan Road in the townland of Lismore).

The Jail Wall disaster on 4 March 1943 led to the deaths of ten people due to the collapse of a wall of the closed jail, which was being used to store fuel. This event will be explored in more depth in Chapter 7.

Ballybricken also staged numerous political rallies, from Daniel O'Connell and Charles Stewart Parnell to John Redmond, whose local support base was formed by the pig buyers from the area.

THE MEDIEVAL MONASTERIES OF WATERFORD

The four main monasteries of medieval Waterford were Blackfriars (Dominicans), Greyfriars (Franciscans), St John's Priory (Benedictine) and St Catherine's (Augustinian), the latter of which was situated at the location of the present-day courthouse. During the 1840s, when excavating the foundations of St Catherine's during the building of the courthouse, a vault was found where a fully preserved body wearing religious robes was uncovered before disintegrating to dust. A ring remained intact, bearing a coat of arms, and was exhibited by the Royal Society of Antiquaries of Ireland in 1858. However, our focus will be on the Dominican and Franciscan friaries, whose ruins are prominent in the city centre to this day.

BLACKFRIARS DOMINICAN PRIORY

The only existing remains are the chancel of the church and the belfry. The entrance to the former is through an arched doorway, highly ornamented with rope mouldings and surmounted by a spacious window; the interior consists of two apartments, low and gloomy, with vaulted roofs supported on groined arches. The belfry is a lofty square tower of massive thickness, having a staircase leading to the summit, from which is obtained an interesting view, especially over the old portion of the city.

Samuel Lewis, *A Topographical Dictionary of Ireland* (1837)

The Dominican priory known as Blackfriars (due to the black *cappa* or cloak worn by the order) was built around 1230 between the old and new city walls. The remains of it today are the shell of the church and bell tower. The Dominicans came to the city in 1226 and were gifted the site of the priory by the citizens of Waterford. The order created schools and educated the sons of wealthy merchants who lived in the city. In 1540, the priory was dissolved by Henry VIII and was later used as a courthouse (from 1617) and became a theatre in 1746.

GREYFRIARS FRANCISCAN FRIARY

Greyfriars Franciscan friary, one of the oldest Franciscan friaries in Ireland, was built in 1241. The walls of the friary are adorned with figures of birds in tribute to the founder of the order, St Francis of the Assisi, and his love of animals. The Franciscan Friary was established by Sir Hugh Purcell (perhaps on behalf of King Henry III) whose grandfather was a lieutenant to Strongbow, who led the Anglo-Norman invasion of Ireland in 1170. The royal connection may have aided the locating of the Franciscan friary in the centre of the Viking Triangle close to Reginald's Tower.

King Richard II visited Waterford in 1394 and held court at Greyfriars. It was the location where four prominent Irish chieftains submitted to the rule of the king. The Medieval church was decorated with a large crucifix which divided the chancel from the congregation. There were altars devoted to the Virgin Mary and the three Magi. A statue of St Christopher, the patron saint of travellers, also furnished the church. The thirteenth-century triple lancets on the east gable are the narrow windows with a pointed arch that can still be seen today. The Lady Chapel of the friary dates to the late thirteenth century with its trefoil-headed lancet topped by a circular light now encasing the 'King of the Vikings', the world's first Viking virtual reality experience.

The friary was closed in 1540 by King Henry VIII when he severed his links with the Church in Rome. It was gifted to Master Patrick Walsh in September 1541 and became the site of an almshouse known as the Holy Ghost Hospital. A year later, a section of the precinct was given to David Baliff, which more than likely led to the creation of Bailey's New Street between the friary and Reginald's Tower.

Greyfriars was an asylum for the poor in the seventeenth century, and the east end of the friary was recommissioned as a church for Huguenots (French Protestants) leading to it being known as French Church. The Franciscan Friary was later used as a hospital well into the nineteenth century.

STEPHEN DE FULBOURNE, BISHOP OF WATERFORD

In 1274, Stephen de Fulbourne, a member of the order of the Knights Hospitallers, was elected Bishop of Waterford and made treasurer of Ireland by King Edward I. By 1281 he held this post with the role of governor or justiciar and appointed family members to important positions in the Irish Chancery. He established mints in Dublin and Waterford; as revenue trebled, both closed due to lack of silver. It seems De Fulbourne pocketed a fair amount of money for himself through bribes and owed over £33,000 to the royal revenue. This led to him being relieved of his duties as treasurer, but he remained as governor and bishop of Waterford. He was succeeded by his brother as bishop in 1286. In Waterford's Medieval Museum one can view Choristers' Hall, built around 1270 by Stephen de Fulbourne as a dwelling

The Choristers' Hall was built in 1270 by Stephen de Fulbourne, Bishop of Waterford. The Englishman was a member of the Order of Knights Hospitallers and twice served as the Lord Justice of Ireland. *Courtesy of Waterford Treasures*

for the dean of the cathedral. Built against the town wall, what now forms the gable end of the building is the thirteenth-century city defences.

THE UNITED DIOCESE OF WATERFORD AND LISMORE

Thomas le Reve became the first bishop of the amalgamated diocese of Waterford and Lismore in 1363. This union was a result of the Norman influence on Ireland. The small diocese of Viking Waterford was dwarfed by the larger more wealthy diocese of Lismore. In fact, Pope John XXII ordered for the union of these two dioceses in 1327 upon the resignation or death of one of the two bishops. However, the then bishop of Waterford, Roger Craddock, had enraged the Archbishop of Cashel with his behaviour and was continually blocked from becoming Bishop of Waterford and Lismore, the honour of which fell to le Reve nearly forty years after it was first decreed.

3

URBS INTACTA MANET WATERFORDIA:
Late Medieval Waterford

TIMELINE

1368 CE: The combined forces of the O'Driscolls and Powers defeat the citizens of Waterford.

1394 CE: King Richard II lands at Waterford.

1413 CE: The O'Driscoll and his six sons are captured by the Mayor of Waterford, Simon Wicken. They are taken to Waterford as hostages and eventually released after their ransom is paid.

1463 CE: A parliament sits in Waterford and leads to a mint being established at Reginald's Tower.

1482 CE: The tomb of James Rice in Christ Church is consecrated by the Bishop of Ossory.

1497 CE: King Henry VII confers the title of *Urbs Intacta Manet* on Waterford, acknowledging how its citizens had resisted the pretenders to the throne of Lambert Simmel and Perkin Warbeck. He also granted the city a new charter.

> *Waterford* [with] *no more than seven acres of land within its walls is like a little castle.*
>
> Petition to King Edward III from Mayor William Lombard, 1371

The city of Waterford strived to regain the previous state of prosperity it enjoyed in the thirteenth and fourteenth centuries but to no avail, due in part to the effects of the Hundred Years' War on trade.

THE GREAT CHARTER ROLL OF WATERFORD:
a Great Treasure of Medieval Ireland

Now for a more detailed look at one of the great gems of medieval Ireland: the Great Charter Roll of Waterford. It contains illustrations of English monarchs from Henry II, the first English king to set foot in Ireland, to Edward III who was on the throne when the roll was compiled. It was presented by Waterford Corporation to King Edward III to aid their case in the city's dispute with the neighbouring port of New Ross.

The Great Charter Roll of Waterford is a unique treasure of medieval Ireland. It was used to illustrate Waterford's superior claim to ships unloading their cargo in the city rather than at New Ross. The dispute was finally concluded in 1518. *Courtesy of Waterford Treasures*

Waterford's position as a royal city led to it having a monopoly on the import of wine to the south-east region of the island. However, the establishment of a port in close proximity at New Ross in 1207 was the start of the longest trade dispute in Irish history. The quarrel became particularly severe during the years of the Black Death, which instigated economic decline. The city of Waterford sought to maintain its status as a significant port in the area.

The charter roll is made up of documents related to the trade dispute with New Ross. However, the officials of the city engaged with artists to illustrate these documents to grab King Edward III's attention and highlight Waterford's loyalty to the crown. The top of the Great Charter Roll is a depiction of the walled city of Waterford and is the oldest image of an Irish city in existence. Over this illustration is an image of the king giving a sword of justice to the mayor, who oversaw the carrying out of justice in the name of the crown. It also signifies the role of the mayor in maintaining the defence of Waterford against the enemies of the English monarchy.

King Edward III, enthroned from the Great Charter Roll of Waterford, 1373. The Roll contains illustrations of English monarchs from Henry II, the first English king to set foot in Ireland, to Edward III who was on the throne when the roll was compiled. *Courtesy of Waterford Treasures*

These depictions of four mayors of the royal cities of Cork, Dublin, Limerick and Waterford are the earliest images of medieval mayors in the islands of Britain and Ireland. These were used to highlight how weakening Waterford's claim would impact the other royal cities as well. The portrayal of seven kings with their being two depictions of Edward III exhibited the loyalty of Waterford to the crown dating back to 1171. The images of Edward III are the only ones still in existence to have been created during his lifetime.

There are also the portraits of eight governors of Ireland from 1221 to 1372, who enforced the exclusion of foreign vessels landing at New Ross. The aim of the Great Charter Roll was to display the precedence of Waterford's claim as a royal city port which outstripped that of its near neighbours, who in essence had been circumventing the law for well over a century and a half.

The dispute finally came to an end in 1518 when the citizens of Waterford sacked New Ross and seized the town's civic mace, which can still be seen in Waterford at the Medieval Museum.

BATTLE OF JOHN'S BRIDGE, 1386

Such conflict can also be seen at the Battle of John's Bridge in 1386. That year, the citizens of Waterford sought an alleviation in payment of tax to King Edward III because they were under siege. One of the groups that aimed to plunder the city was the Powers. In retaliation to a robbery near Waterford, the mayor, John Malpas, led an attack at the location of the incident at Cloncamanmore, but he and his men were ambushed. The Powers, sensing that the city was at a low ebb, attempted to breach its defences. Led by Richard Mór Poer, they attacked John's Bridge, where the city's mayor, the Baron of Dunhill and his brother Bennett all died in the conflict. The attack was not only the summit of Power attacks on Waterford but also resulted in the end of the Powers of Dunhill.

KING RICHARD II AND WATERFORD CITY

In 1394, Richard II, in the seventeenth year of his reign, arrived in Waterford on 2 October. His aim was to restore order to Ireland and add a semblance of respect to his reign, which was largely uninspiring. He held the aims of 'the punishment and correction of our rebels there, and to establish good government, and just rule over our faithful lieges'. The party of 30,000 archers and 4,000 soldiers traversed the island for eight months and he held court at Greyfriars, where the Irish princes submitted to the rule of the English monarch. The following policies were instigated: with the 'Wild Irish' the idea of 'Surrender and Regrant' was followed (a policy later adopted by Henry VIII) where they would become subjects of the king; and the descendants of the Normans who had now gone native were also made to comply with the orders of the royal. This was a major change in course of English policy in Ireland as the king sought to amalgamate the 'Wild' and 'rebel' Irish as one nation.

The local affairs of the city continued uninhibited by the Dublin government, due in part to the latter's inadequacies, into the reign of King Henry IV, with the Mayor of Waterford receiving special conditions.

Around the fifteenth century, New Street and New Gate were created, running to the area where Barrack Street is located today. Medieval Waterford encompassed round 53 acres, with a rough estimate of the city's population being about 5,000 inhabitants. The defences of the city numbered fifteen gateways and twenty-three towers, which were certainly needed. Disputes and conflicts related to Waterford in the fourteenth and fifteenth centuries arose from the city's refusal to pay protection money to groups such as the Powers of Dunhill and the O'Driscolls of Baltimore.

Threats like this did not die with the Powers after the battle of John's Bridge in 1386, as noted earlier. In 1461, a battle took place near Ballymacaw where the forces of the city of Waterford captured the leaders of the piratical clan, the O'Driscolls, and three of their galleys. It is possible that these are the three ships which are contained within the coat of arms of the city.

Upon Edward IV rising to the throne, Waterford's affiliation with the crown was strengthened when he issued a charter to the city. The fortunes of Waterford were improving, with a growth in the wool trade combined with investment in local monasteries such as the development of bell towers at both the Franciscan and Dominican friaries in the latter part of the fifteenth century.

WATERFORD AND THE WAR OF THE ROSES

In 1487, Waterford displayed its loyalty to the English throne by refusing to submit to the rule of the pretender to the crown of Henry VII, Lambert Simnel. Simnel was the Yorkist pretender to the English throne during the War of the Roses. He and the Yorkists claimed that he was Edward, Earl of Warwick, who was rival to Henry VII. However, the real Earl of Warwick was a prisoner of Henry and placed on display in London.

An engraving of Lambert Simnel, pretender to the English throne. *Encyclopedia Britannica, 11 ed, Vol. XXV, 1910*

Perkin Warbeck, fifteenth-century drawing. The execution of Warbeck marked the end of the War of the Roses.

On 5 May 1487, Simnel landed in Dublin with an army of 2,000 men and was crowned Edward VI in Christ Church Cathedral on 24 May, though he was opposed by Waterford.

The Earl of Kildare, Gearóid Mór Fitzgerald, was appointed by Simnel as Lord Lieutenant. The Mayor of Waterford sent a messenger to the Earl of Kildare with the information that the city would not support Simnel's claim to the throne. Fitzgerald had the messenger hanged at Thingmote in Dublin and it is suggested that the phrase 'killing the messenger' originates from this event.

The city was besieged in vain in 1495 by Perkin Warbeck, another pretender to the English crown. Warbeck claimed to be Richard IV, Duke of York, the deceased brother of Edward V. He gained support from Charles VII of France and James IV of Scotland in his claim to the throne. In attacking Waterford, it was the first time in which artillery was used in the siege of an Irish city, while the cannons at Reginald's Tower managed to sink one of Warbeck's ships during the eleven-day siege. He returned to England and was captured. Together with John Water, the former Mayor of Cork, he was hanged in 1499. The execution of Warbeck arguably marked the end of the War of the Roses.

The loyalty of the city to the English monarchy was recognised by Henry VII when he bestowed Waterford with the motto *Urbs Intacta Manet Waterfordia* – the city of Waterford remains untaken.

MAYOR'S WINE VAULT AND JAMES RICE

The wine vault was built around 1440 by Peter Rice, who was an affluent wine merchant and mayor of the city. His son James was also a wine merchant and served as Mayor of Waterford eleven times between the years 1476 and 1488. James Rice had a great standing in his native city and abroad. His name is noted in the *Liber Primus,* Rolls of Parliament in London as well as the archives in the Vatican. The younger Rice presented the wine vault and house above it to Dean John Collyn on 6 July 1468 and it became a residence for priests of the new chantry chapel (built by Collyn) until 1520.

The Mayor's Wine Vault dating to the fifteenth century was built by Peter Rice, father of James. It now encompasses part of the Medieval Museum. *Courtesy of Waterford Treasures*

By the fifteenth century, merchants such as James Rice began to source wine from the Iberian Peninsula as the traditional trade was not possible due to the impact of the Hundred Years' War. Twice Rice travelled to Spain on pilgrimage to the shrine of St James the Apostle at Santiago de Compostela. Before his second expedition, Rice had a gothic cadaver tomb built in Christ Church Cathedral where it still can be seen today. It was originally located in a chantry chapel added to Christ Church by Rice in 1482. It was called St James's Chapel but known as Rice's Chapel. Under the decaying effigy of the tomb reads the inscription:

> Here lies James Rice, late citizen of this city, and by his direction is interred Katherine Brown, his wife. Whose thou art that passeth by, stop, read, mourn, I am what thou wilt be, and I was what thou art. Pray for me I beseech thee. It is our lot to pass through the gates of death. We entreat Thee, O Christ, to have mercy on us. We beseech Thee who comest to redeem the lost not to condemn the redeemed.

CLOTH OF GOLD VESTMENTS:
only Full Set of Medieval Vestments to Survive in Northern Europe

The Waterford cloth of gold vestments date to the 1460s and are made from Florentine silk. The panels of the garments were embroidered in Bruges, which was the hub of such needlework in the Middle Ages. Bruges had trading connections with Waterford and served as a link between northern and southern Europe. The robes are decorated with scenes from the Bible and are the only full set of medieval vestments to survive in northern Europe.

As Ireland's only link with the Renaissance, the vestments were fashioned during a period when people sought indulgences for their sins in order to guarantee their passage to heaven. The construction of the chantry chapel was by Dean Collyn, who was a friend of James Rice. It is believed that Rice was more than likely the patron of these vestments.

In the Medieval Museum, one can see three copes (which are large cloaks), two dalmatics (which are T-shaped) and a chasuble. These would

The Waterford cloth of gold vestments date to the 1460s and are the only full set of medieval vestments to survive in northern Europe. *Courtesy of Waterford Treasures*

have been worn by a priest to celebrate Mass for special occasions. They were buried in 1650 as Waterford fell to the forces of the republican army as part of Cromwell's conquest of the island. It was 123 years before they were rediscovered, when the medieval Christ Church was demolished to make way for the new Georgian structure that we can see there today.

An illustration of the veneration in which the Church was held during the late Medieval period can be seen in 1483, when the Waterford Corporation passed a law that decreed parents would be held responsible if their children destroyed the glass windows of churches.

THE QUAY

... indeed is not only the best and most convenient Quay which I have found in Ireland, but it is as good a Quay as I have known either in England, or observed in all my travels ...

Sir William Brereton, 1635

The longest street in Waterford City, the Quay stretches from Adelphi Lane to Bilberry Road. The earliest known reference to the Quay is in 1377 when King Edward III permitted the mayor and bailiffs of the city the customs duty of the

The Quay, Waterford, c. 1890 to c. 1900. *Library of Congress*

port for a decade. The Quay was exposed to attack as the city walls were not repaired, but they were subsequently strengthened due to fear of an attack from the Spanish. In the Medieval period, the 'Great Quay' was crammed between Turgesius' Tower (which is believed to have stood in the area of Barronstrand Street) and Christ Church Lane (now known as Henrietta Street).

The Great Quay was lengthened eastwards towards Reginald's Tower in the sixteenth century. In 1674, it was arranged for the quay and wall to be repaired by the corporation. The following decades saw steady improvements with docks, paving and gates leading to an extension from Barronstrand Street.

The Quay was transformed by changes directed by Mayor David Lewis in 1705, such as the removal of the city wall which ran adjacent to the River Suir. Further extensions east and west of the Quay brought about the street which we are acquainted with today. These developments took place during a prosperous period for the city as the bacon and butter trades grew, with Charles Smith noting in 1746:

The Exchange, together with the Custom House adjoining are charmingly situated on the Kay. The Exchange is a neat light building, supported by pillars of hewn stone of the Tuscan order, the outside being adorned with the arms of the King, and those of the City, with an handsome clock. The roof is an Italian hipt roof, with a beautiful octogon cupulo, and a dome at top; the cupulo being surrounded by a balustrade, about which is a walk. The space below stairs for the merchants to assemble in, is sufficiently large and spacious, on one side whereof is the Town Clerk's Office, separated from the rest. Above stairs are the Council Chamber, and a large Assembly-room besides other apartments. In the Council Chamber is a very large perspective view of the City finely painted by Vanderhagen.

The New Quay was where a glass factory, established in 1783 by George and William Penrose, was located, with some funding from the Irish Parliament. A prominent building of historic significance on the Quay is the Granville Hotel, originally a townhouse which was the birthplace of the Irish patriot Thomas Francis Meagher. It was subsequently purchased by the Italian transport magnate Charles Bianconi, who altered the building to become a hotel and the Waterford depot for his horse-drawn stagecoaches. In 1826, the Quay was lit by gas lighting.

In 1875, construction began of the Custom House and the General Post Office (which was enlarged in 1883 to facilitate parcel post). The Quay was expanded further by 1886, the extension spanning from the bridge to Strangman's brewery and named Grattan Quay. The other sections of the Quay are Adelphi Quay (from the mouth of St John's River to the Mall); Parade Quay (Keizer's Lane to Reginald's Tower); Custom House Quay (Keizer's Lane to Exchange Street); Coal Quay (Exchange Street to Barronstrand Street); Merchant's Quay (Barronstrand Street to Bridge Street) and Meagher's Quay which spans Gladstone Street to Conduit Lane.

The Quay was surfaced with asphalt in 1928, the first time that such a road surfacing material was used in Waterford City.

4

PARVA ROMA – LITTLE ROME:
Waterford in the Sixteenth and Seventeenth Centuries

TIMELINE

1534 CE: William Wyse is elected Mayor of the City of Waterford. In a rebellion lead by (Silken) Thomas Fitzgerald, Wyse allows King Henry VIII to land at Waterford before proceeding to crush the rebellion.

1536 CE: Henry VIII presents William Wyse with a letter of thanks, a sword and a cap which would have been worn beneath the crown of the king. It is one of the oldest such caps surviving in Europe.

1538 CE: The O'Driscolls' base in Baltimore in County Cork is attacked and destroyed by the forces of Waterford City, ending two centuries of feuding.

1546 CE: The Holy Ghost Hospital at Greyfriars is established after Henry Walsh is granted a patent by Henry VIII.

1554 CE: Peter Lombard is born. Lombard subsequently becomes the Archbishop of Armagh.

1588 CE: Luke Wadding is born on 16 October.

1603 CE: Upon the succession of James I after the death of Elizabeth I, the citizens of Waterford reinstate Catholic worship and hold Masses. The Lord Deputy Mountjoy, with the royal army, arrives at the city but is refused entry by its citizens under the provisions of the charter of King John from 1215.

1625 CE: Charles I grant the citizens of Waterford a new charter in return for £3,000. The Mayor of Waterford is bestowed the title of Admiral of the Port.

1649 CE: Cromwell besieges Waterford but fails to capture it.

1650 CE: Waterford City is surrendered by General Preston to the commander of Cromwell's army, General Ireton.

1652 CE: The Act of Settlement in Ireland is printed in Waterford.

1654 CE: It is ordered that no Papists are allowed to trade in the city.

1656 CE: It is decreed that all Quakers should be rounded up and sent to Bristol.

1678 CE: The Lord Lieutenant and Council order that all Roman Catholics in the city be removed except those of vital importance.

1688 CE: A new charter to the Roman Catholic citizens of Waterford is granted by King James II.

1690 CE: After defeat at the Battle of the Boyne, King James arrives in Waterford before sailing for France from Duncannon in County Wexford. Later in the month, William of Orange enters the city.

1693 CE: A resolution is passed by Waterford Corporation that provisions be made for the arrival of fifty French Protestant (Huguenot) families.

1696 CE: The city's medieval defences are dismantled and replaced by three- and four-storey houses along the Quay, known as 'Dutch Billies' as their design was influenced by the Dutch style.

This city of Waterford much flourisheth and I suppose was never in better estate since it was builded, the people thereof being very civil, and (for this country) full of industry.

Sir Henry Sidney, 1567

Waterford is the second city in Ireland. It is a loyal and well administered municipality, full of honest and prudent citizens, but not particularly well lit because of the narrowness of the streets. Its sheltered port is usually crowded with foreign ships. A large number of the citizens are engaged in trade and their thrifty book-keeeping results in their amassing great wealth over a short space of time. The bulk of their commerce is with Spain. For the most part they use their own coins rather than foreign currency. One finds no dishonest bankers there who deal fraudently in currency exchange or cheat the people by charging intolerable usury, which is the downfall of all states. The citizens are friendly, generous, hospitable, frugal and adept in their public and private affairs.

Richard Stanihurst, *De Rebus in Hibernia gestis*, 1584

The Gentle Shure, which passing sweet Clonmel, Adorns rich Waterford.

William Spenser, *The Faerie Queen*, 1590

Waterford is situated upon the best harbour and her beauty is in the Quay.

Luke Gernon, Second Justice of Munster, 1620

WATERFORD CITY IN THE TUDOR PERIOD

In 1510, Henry VII granted Waterford a charter which contains the earliest known image of the city's coat of arms. The Reformation and subsequent dissolution of the monasteries saw the Franciscan Friary at Greyfriars come under the ownership of the Walsh family, who were local to Waterford. The friary was converted to an almshouse in 1544 and named the Holy Ghost Hospital. Some churches and monasteries in the city were destroyed. Though the wealthy families complied with the Act of Supremacy of Henry VIII, many such as the Walshes appreciated the old Catholic traditions and managed to save religious statues that previously adorned churches in Waterfor d.

The defences of the city were strengthened for the first time since the thirteenth century by Henry VIII. In 1574, the Spanish spy Don Diego Ortiz noted that 'the city contains nearly a thousand houses. It is surrounded by a stone wall, something less than a mile in circumference, with seventeen towers, and cannon on them to keep off savages. It is the richest town in Ireland after Dublin.'

The dissolution of monasteries freed up space within the city, which already struggled to remain inside its protected boundaries.

Above left: Representations of the coat of arms of Waterford City taken from Ryland's *The history, topography and antiquities of the county and city of Waterford* published in 1824. The symbol of the three ships evokes the maritime importance of the city. Some commentators believe that it relates to the inhabitants of Waterford capturing three galleys of the O'Driscolls in 1467. The representation of three lions dates to the reign of Queen Elizabeth I. *British Library*

Above right: The motto of the city, Urbs Intacta Manet, was conferred by Henry VII in 1497 in appreciation to Waterford's resolve and loyalty to the crown against the forces of Lambert Simnel and Perkin Warbeck. *British Library*

The development of larger timber-framed houses in the sixteenth and seventeenth centuries within the confines of the thirteenth-century city walls exacerbated this problem.

The loyalty of the city to the English crown began to waiver upon the ascension of Elizabeth I to the throne and the reforms she wanted to introduce to the Church. Local merchants had developed a fidelity to Rome and the Catholic Church due to Waterford's ability to trade with continental Europe. Once more, the city's defences were strengthened with the building of St Patrick's Fort outside the city walls to monitor and manage the passage of the River Suir. A map dating to the late sixteenth century shows a blockhouse for cannon in front of Reginald's Tower.

Waterford was a landing point for government forces during the Nine Years' War (1593–1603). Sir Henry Norreys entered the city with 2,000 soldiers in 1598 before laying siege to the town of Cahir in County Tipperary. The stationing of such large numbers of soldiers is believed to have led to the spread of plague, with 256 deaths being detailed for the year ending September 1604.

The death of Queen Elizabeth was greeted as a return to Catholic practices in Waterford, with the local clergy precipitously taking control of the cathedral and churches that were previously given to Protestants. The Dublin government made sure that the circumstances which Elizabeth instigated remained after her death. Yet Waterford refused to submit to the Oath of Supremacy of King James on religious grounds, which led to the Corporation of Waterford being suspended in 1618. For the duration of James' reign, Waterford was ruled by government officials and its charters taken to Dublin.

THE INVASION OF NEW ROSS, MAY 1518

There was a rivalry between New Ross in County Wexford and the city of Waterford over trade for well over 250 years. Both shared the same estuary to the sea, but under royal charters, vessels were to by-pass New Ross and land at Waterford, where the king was to receive two pipes of wine in taxes. However, this was not obeyed by the dwellers of the Wexford town. By 1267, up to forty ships had been detained at New Ross, which was a not unsubstantial loss to the revenue of the city. In 1518, the Mayor of Waterford, Patrick Roche, led a fleet made up of the city's inhabitants, French and Spanish sailors which attacked New Ross. They inflicted around £100 worth of damage and were given a silver gilt mace to end the invasion.

HENRY VIII'S CAP OF MAINTENANCE:
a Mark of Royal Approval

Gifted to the Mayor of Waterford by King Henry VIII in 1536, the cap is made from red velvet from Lucca in Italy. Baleen from whale is used to strengthen the cap. It is embroidered with gold bullion for a Tudor rose on the flat of the cap with daisies on the brim. The cap is a considerable symbol of royal approval for Waterford and is the only piece of clothing belonging to the king to have survived the centuries.

Above left: Portrait of Henry VIII by Hans Holbein, *c.* 1537 to 1547.

Above right: King Henry VIII's Cap of Maintenance was a gift from the king to the Mayor of Waterford in 1536. It is the only piece of Henry VIII's wardrobe to survive in the world. *Courtesy of Waterford Treasures*

Henry VIII's personal connection to Waterford was that his childhood friend William Wyse grew up in the royal court. William was invited to the court in recognition of his father John's loyalty to the reign of Henry VII. William Wyse was ambassador to the royal court in 1536 and was tasked with bringing the Cap of Maintenance and a sword to the city. It was a gift from the king to Waterford for remaining loyal to the crown during the rebellion of 1534 in Ireland.

The king had bestowed three charters to the city, while William Wyse also benefitted personally from his connections with the monarch. Upon the dissolution of the monasteries by Henry VIII, William Wyse received 1000 acres of church land from the disbanding of such religious institutions.

LIBER ANTIQUISSIMUS CIVITATIS WATERFORDIAE – The Great Parchment Book

The Great Parchment Book of Waterford holds the records of the city from 1356 to 1649 and consists of 233 vellum sheets. The first section of the book goes from 1356 to the 1470s and was the result of Mayor James Rice's rearranging of the records of the city. Each year is chronicled under the name of the Mayor of Waterford for that year and the reigning monarch.

On the 1556 page, there are a series of illustrations which are an assertion of the religious beliefs of the citizens of Waterford during the reign of Queen Elizabeth I. There are the royal arms above the walled city of Port Láirge, which is the only Irish used in the document. One can see on the top right of the page a depiction of God holding a sword and bordered by the Archangels Gabriel and Michael, passing judgement on souls in Purgatory on Armageddon, one of which is that of the queen. There are banners which state in Latin, *judge wisely* and *remember death*.

There is an image of the Virgin Mary who is suckling the baby Jesus, a statement rejecting the Protestant doctrine of the Virgin Queen of England. The image of the Virgin is one of only two to survive in Ireland (the other is in the manuscript of the Book of Kells). The pagan image of the Green Man is also present, possibly as a missive to the English monarch to revert to the old religion rather than creating a new form of paganism.

The last entry in 1649 of the Great Parchment Book notes the mayor as John Levitt and the king as Charles I. When the English king was executed, his son Charles is recorded as king but the page was later defaced when Cromwell's army took the city.

PETER LOMBARD:
Absentee Archbishop of Armagh

Born in Waterford around 1554, Peter Lombard studied at Oxford and Louvain in Belgium. At the latter university he became a professor of philosophy and theology.

In Rome around 1598–99, Lombard functioned as an agent for Hugh O'Neill to Pope Clement VIII. Clement appointed the Waterford man to the position of Archbishop of Armagh. While in the Eternal City, he wrote *De Regno Hiberniae Sanctorum Insula – observation on the kingdom of Ireland, island of saints* (which wasn't published until 1633 and was suppressed by Charles I).

Lombard was conservative and denounced the theories of Copernicus. He died in Rome in 1625.

'THE CITY OF WATERFORD MUCH FLOURISHETH':
Sir Henry Sidney's Views of Sixteenth-Century Waterford

Under the reign of Queen Elizabeth, one of the more notable Lord Deputies was Sir Henry Sidney. In an attempt to impose order on the island (without the necessary financial resources) he made numerous excursions across the country, the first of which began in January 1567. He arrived at Waterford via Clonmel, County Tipperary. He noted the loyalty of the city to the queen as well as the problem the Powers dealt to them. Yet the latter contended that their lands were under threat and their actions were merely defence. Sidney attempted to settle that matter and remarked, 'The city of Waterford much flourisheth, and I suppose was never in better estate since it was builded, the people thereof being very civil and (for this country) full of industry.' He left Waterford for Dungarvan towards Youghal. Sidney served three periods as Lord Deputy from 1565 to 1578, promoting the Tudor reconquest.

Sir Henry Sidney by Arnold Bronckorst (1573).

A SEA-DOG IN THE SOUTH-EAST:
Sir Thomas Stucley and Waterford

Sir Thomas Stucley was a Roman Catholic recusant who posed continuous problems for successive monarchs of the English throne. The Devon man spread the rumour that he was the illegitimate son of King Henry VIII. A pioneer of the English Tudor 'sea-dog', Stucley served as a soldier on the Scottish border before subsequently becoming a licenced privateer during the reign of Mary Tudor.

Stucley's pirating saw him become familiar with the southern ports of Ireland. John de Courcy, a research officer with the Maritime Institute of Ireland, wrote of Sir Thomas Stucley that he was the:

> first person clearly to appreciate the vital importance of Ireland's strategic situation in the newly-emerging Atlantic orientated Europe of the mid-16th century. Ireland was no longer an island of marginal significance on the outer edge of inward-looking Europe. It had become the key to controlling a Europe whose destinies had suddenly and irrevocably become dependent on the navigation of the Atlantic Ocean.

It would appear that Stucley's first visit to Waterford was late in the summer of 1563, when he brought his plunder of two French ships from La Rochelle, with the booty sold on the quayside. The scandal led the Spanish Ambassador in London to correspond with Queen Elizabeth's Secretary of State seeking redress. The secretary wrote to the Lord Deputy of Ireland pressing for the matter to be resolved.

In 1565, the Lord Justice Nicholas Arnold ordered for Stucley to be apprehended and brought to the Town Hall in the city. The privateer could not be penalised as no witness would come forward to confirm that he had sold pirated goods. Over the next two years he increased his influence in Ireland by buying properties in Wexford and sought to have some form of control over the affairs of Waterford, which he believed would be a significant location in his enterprise. A feud developed between Stucley and Sir Peter Carew over some of the lands acquired by the former in Wexford. The Devon native sought to have Carew assassinated but was arrested before being released, and went to Waterford.

Stucley began a dialogue with the King of Spain and presented plans to have Spanish soldiers and warships reach Waterford and start an invasion of England. In 1570, he set sail for Spain with cannons, believed to have been taken from the city walls of Waterford, as a gift for the Spanish monarch. Upon his arrival at Cantabria, Stucley proclaimed himself the Duke of Ireland and opposer of the English occupation of Ireland. There was a plan for the Spanish Armada to invade Waterford in 1574 (the Spanish spy Diego Ortiz had provided reconnaissance on the defences of the city), but this never took place due to conflict with the Turks' siege of Tunis. Of this, John de Courcy concludes that 'no man in military or naval history has been more concerned with the importance of Waterford than Thomas Stucley'.

TOPOGRAPHICALLY SPEAKING:
Maps and Plans of Waterford

The National Library of Ireland's collection holds the oldest map of Waterford, titled *The true description of the City of Waterford and the new fortification there, also the fort of the rock, the true course of the river, the new works at Passage and the fortification at Duncannon erected in anno-1591*. It was drawn by Francis Jobson in 1591 and includes the entirety of Waterford Harbour with the 'new fortification' possibly being a reference to the extension to the city wall. The map focuses on works of defence.

A new fortification built in the seventeenth century was the Citadel or St Patrick's Fort planned by Josias Bodley, replacing an unfinished fort by Edmund Yoke which began in 1590. Bodley died in 1617 and was succeeded by Capt. Nicholas Pynnar to complete the project. The document *The Report of Captain Nicholas Pynnar, how far forth he hath proceeded towards the finishing of the Fort at Waterford as appeareth by his letter to the Council of War dated the 26th December, 1626* outlines the completion of construction of the fort with walls 6ft in thickness and a rampart 25ft in width.

The Down Survey of 1654–56 was a baronial survey of Ireland undertaken by Sir William Petty to aid the distribution of land for the re-conquest of Ireland after the Confederate War. The surveyor for County Waterford was Francis Cooper whose name figures on the map of the Liberties of Waterford, which illustrates 'places of eminency' in the city of Waterford such as the ruins of the Abbey of St Katherine, the house and castle at Gracedieu and Kilbarry. There are also references to the settlements at Ballytruckle, Grange and Newtown. Ballybricken is noted as the 'Great Green' while there was a common green where Barrack Street is located today. There are sixty-four place names in total documented on the map.

Ryland's history of Waterford (published in 1824) reproduced a semi-pictorial map of the city at it was in 1673. It would appear to be a copy of an early map which was lost. Notable features include the battery located by Reginald's Tower, St John's Fort outside the city wall, John's Bridge being the only bridge over St John's River, the Pill and the Market Cross. The latter is described by J.S. Carroll as 'a very nice feature, consisting of a stepped pedestal on which stood the cross under a dome supported by four columns'.

There is a map dating to 1685 drafted by Sir Thomas Philips, a military engineer to Charles II, for military purposes. There are very few details of the interior of the city, though the city walls and defences are vividly shown. In total there are twenty-five towers, while Reginald's Tower is labelled as a 'Storehouse'. It also shows John's Bridge as being a drawbridge.

1673 map of Waterford. *M-PV-72, Waterford City & County Archives*

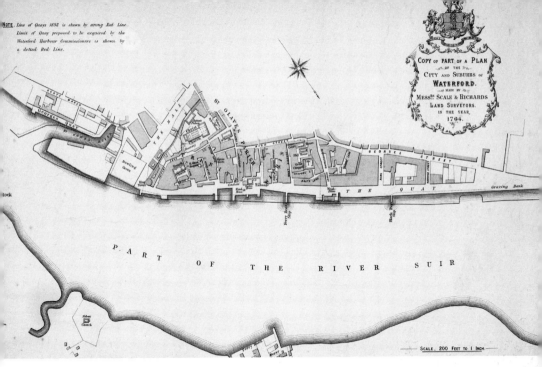

Richards and Scale map of 1764. *M-PV-71, Waterford City & County Archives*

Around 1691, there is a map entitled the *Plan de la Ville et Citadelle de Waterford* by the Huguenot Jean Goubet who served in the Williamite army, and the map is dedicated to the Duke of Wittenberg.

Charles Smith's history of the city published in 1745 carries an illustrative map but fails to attribute the person who drew it. The city wall along the Quay is gone, the Citadel is now a barrack, the creation of the Mall and Bailey's New Street appears. There is a bowling green at the top of the Mall while a second one is located at the present site of Morris's. Ballybricken Green is noted as the Fair Place. There is also a second bridge spanning St John's River at Lombard Street (a drawbridge). There is a Fish House situated where the Clock Tower now stands. There is the creation of the Mayor's Walk near Ballybricken, named in honour of Simon Newport, the mayor.

In 1764, there is the William Richards and Benjamin Scale map of the city but it does not present any new features or great detail compared to that outlined in Smith's history. Though there are some new street names, with William Street as Scots Marsh, there is Rose Lane and Beau Walk, while Bailey's New Street is labelled Factory Lane and Greyfriars is Holy Ghost Lane. The Quaker Meeting House was located at the site of the Christian

Leahy map of the city and surrounding townlands of 1834. *M-PV-35, Waterford City & County Archives*

Brother school on Manor Street. A deer park and ornamental gardens of Alderman Dr Francis Barker are present on the map, covering the area of the present Barker Street, Francis Street, Jail Street, Meeting House Lane, Thomas's Hill and Wellington Street.

On the P. Leahy map of 1834 one can see the bridge by Lemuel Cox on the River Suir for the first time. New buildings include the Town Hall, the Artillery and Infantry Barracks, the Fever Hospital and Gandon's Courthouse at Ballybricken. There are now four bridges crossing the Pill.

In 1839, the Royal Engineers under the direction of Lieut. Larcom devised maps of Irish towns and cities for the Boundary Commission, which led to the introduction of the Municipal Corporations Act which saw the boundary of Waterford trimmed. These maps were published between 1840 and 1841.

Under the Towns Improvements Clauses Act 1854, local authorities had to keep their own large-scale maps. The Ordnance Survey map of Waterford (at a scale of 5 feet to 1 mile) appeared in 1871 with a revised edition completed by 1908.

LUKE WADDING, FRANCISCAN SCHOLAR WHO CREATED ST PATRICK'S DAY

Luke Wadding was born on 16 October 1588 in Waterford. His father was Walter, a wealthy merchant whose wife was Anastasia (née Lombard, a relative of the Archbishop of Armagh Peter Lombard). He was also related to David Rothe, the Bishop of Ossary and Patrick Comerford, Bishop of Waterford. Wadding was the eleventh of fourteen children (ten boys and four girls). Luke is believed to have been educated at John Flahy's school in Waterford, learning classics and logic. The school managed by White and Flahy in Waterford had been described as a 'Trojan horse', as Jesuit and Francophile influence was implicit in Catholic education.

After the death of his parents in 1602, Luke Wadding was brought by his brother Matthew to Lisbon, Portugal, and entered the Irish college there as a seminarian in 1603. After studying in Lisbon and Coimbra he joined the Franciscan Order.

In 1617, Wadding was president of the Irish college at Salamanca and a year later became theologian to the Spanish embassy in Rome. In Rome, he promoted the doctrine of the Immaculate Conception which did not form part of Catholic teaching until 1854 when it was authorised by Pope Pius IX.

The Waterford man established the Irish Franciscan College of St Isidore in Rome and supported similar developments at Louvain and Prague. Some of his notable works include the eight-volume history of the Franciscan order

Luke Wadding (1731) was an Irish Franciscan friar and historian who established St Patrick's Day as a feast day. Portrait by Andrea Rossi

Statue of Luke Wadding situated by Greyfriars, the ruins of the Franciscan Friary. *Author photograph*

titled *Annales Minorum* (which he started in 1625 and completed in 1654) and a twelve-volume study on Duns Scotus, who Wadding claimed to be Irish. Edel Bhreathnach, the coordinator of *Louvain 400* at the University College Dublin Mícheál Ó Cléirigh Institute for the Study of Irish History and Civilisation, in 2007 noted that Wadding is 'regarded as the father of the history of the Franciscans to this day'. Such is his significance the archive of the General Order in Rome is named in his honour.

Wadding remained in Rome for the rest of his life. During the Confederate Wars he convinced Pope Innocent X to provide weapons and funds to Owen Rua O'Neill in 1642, which gave rise to his reputation as 'a gun-running priest'. During the Papal conclaves of 1644 and 1655, Wadding received votes to be elected Pope but was unsuccessful. He was also pivotal in the appointment of Giovanni Battista Rinuccini as nuncio in 1645.

One of Wadding's lasting legacies is the adding of St Patrick's feast day on 17 March to the liturgical calendar. He died on 18 November 1657, refusing all church honours.

THE CITADEL/ST PATRICK'S FORT

The Citadel, also known as St Patrick's Fort, was located by St Patrick's Gate (where the Garda Station is today). The earliest known reference to the fort is in 1590 when it is recorded that Edmund Yorke, a military engineer, was tasked with building such a fortification. In 1615, it is recounted that soldiers based at the fort took timbers from St Patrick's Church for firewood. Ten years later, Sir Thomas Botheram and Captain Nicholas Pynnar were charged with the construction of a new fort which, when completed, could accommodate 120 men. It combined the three existing towers of the city's defences.

Charles Smith, in his history of the city, in 1746 wrote:

> Where the barracks now stand on St Thomas's Hill, was anciently a square fort consisting of four bastions and curtains, mounted with great guns and encompassed with a moat, except on the side next the town wall, and that side whereon the gate of barracks now stands. By the bastion next to St Patrick's Gate, there was a communication between the fort and the town, on which stood an iron gate. On the north side of this fort towards the river were several out-works, as ravelins, half-moons, etc., and this piece of fortification served the town as a citadel.

Today one can see sections of the Citadel that still survive, such as the north bastion and north-west corner overlooking King's Terrace which stands at 3m in height.

MOUNTJOY IN WATERFORD, 1603

The citizens of Waterford were elated upon the death of Queen Elizabeth in 1603, as Protestantism had been the official religion and the city's trade had been devastated by the war with Spain under her reign. With the arrival of King James I, it was believed that Catholicism would receive a more lenient response from the monarchy. Such was this renewed belief and hope that a Mass led by the Pope's representative Dr James White was held at St Patrick's and the cathedral. Since it was seen as an insult to the royal power, the Lord Deputy, Lord Charles Mountjoy, arrived near the city with an army of 5,000 men that May. However, they were not permitted crossing by ferry from Grannagh to Waterford by its citizens. A stand-off ensued, and Mountjoy was met by Dr White and a Cistercian monk named Father Thomas Lombard where it was agreed that the Lord Deputy would enter the city the following day. In return, the churches would be given back to the Protestants while private Masses were permitted. There was no further retribution from Mountjoy.

THE ABOLITION OF WATERFORD CORPORATION, 1618

By 1600, Waterford was still considered the second city of Ireland, with a prominent harbour and quay being Ireland's gateway to Europe. The city could accommodate ships of 300 tons on its quayside. However, the O'Neill wars (which the city wasn't consistent in) would lessen Waterford's status, with the city's charter being withheld from 1617 to 1626. Stanihurst deemed the citizens of Waterford to be suspicious, restrained and affluent. Julian Walton describes 'the very idea of subjects being loyal to the King in politics but to the Pope in religion was inconceivable to the seventeenth-century mind, and that made trouble inevitable'. This was the case in relation to the citizens of Waterford and King James I. The king had granted the city a new charter in 1609, which appeared to herald a new era of prosperity after the difficult years endured under the reign of Elizabeth. In fact, the opposite occurred. The year 1616 saw the twelfth mayor elected in five years. This number was due to many of them failing to take the Oath of Supremacy to the king as the head of the Church. Eventually, Walter Cleere, a Protestant, was elected mayor (and one of his sheriffs was a Jew named Zabulon Beirg) in 1617. However, they did not have enough time to restore order to Waterford before the citizens elected another Catholic mayor. The government issued a warrant to obtain the charters of the city and thus abolished the Waterford Corporation in 1618.

CHARITABLE INSTITUTIONS OF OLD WATERFORD

There was a Free School of Christ Church Cathedral which was part of the Protestant cathedral established well before the Reformation. It was funded by the local corporation, with one of the noteworthy teachers being a Mr Fagan, who was deemed a 'jolly schoolmaster'.

Located on Stephen Street at the corner of Bachelor's Walk was the Catholic University School, previously Price's School – a Protestant Grammar School. It was acquired by Bishop Dominic O'Brien in 1665 and became the Catholic University under the influence of Cardinal Newman.

WATERFORD AND THE ENGLISH CIVIL WAR, 1642–51

The years between 1641 and 1653 saw the Irish Confederate Wars or the Eleven Years' War take place where indigenous Catholics clashed with English and Scottish Protestant settlers. The victor of the wars was the English Parliament but Waterford had backed the Confederate Catholics of Ireland. Upon the outbreak of the war in 1641, Waterford allowed the Catholic Confederate army of Lord Mountgarret into the city and remained under Confederate command until 1650 when it fell to the army of the English Parliament. A letter from the period to the Franciscan friar Luke Wadding sees Waterford referred to as *Parva Roma* ('Little Rome') due to its loyalty to the Catholic Church and the number of important Catholic scholars from the city.

On 24 November 1649, Oliver Cromwell reached the outskirts of the city, commencing a siege which lasted nine days. It ended due to a mixture of bad weather, lack of artillery and an outbreak of dysentery among Cromwellian forces. A cannonball from this siege is still lodged in the wall of Reginald's Tower. Waterford subsequently surrendered to English Parliament forces led by Cromwell's son-in-law Henry Ireton in August 1650. A Protestant-centred corporation was formed with Catholics now on the periphery in governing the affairs of the city. Many Catholics were dispossessed of their land with some being transported as indentured slaves to Barbados.

After the Restoration, however, things improved for the Catholics in Waterford. The latter years of the kingship of Charles II saw several Catholics conferred as freemen of the city, which permitted them to work as merchants. Waterford Corporation commissioned Edmund Russell, a silversmith, to create copper tokens which would be used in the city. In 1685, upon the succession of James II to the throne, Waterford was granted a new charter which permitted the corporation of the city to elect representatives to the Westminster

Oliver Cromwell. *Wikimedia Commons*

parliament. In the latter half of the seventeenth century, the corporation had a Catholic majority, but further developments were impeded when in July 1690 the city surrendered to the Protestant King William of Orange. The prompt submission of the city saw it gain sympathetic terms; however, Waterford Corporation would not have another Catholic member until the middle of the nineteenth century in Thomas Wyse.

'I SHALL TAKE WATERFORD BY HOOK OR BY CROOKE!':
Cromwellian Siege of Waterford, 1649

Oliver Cromwell planned to start his invasion of Ireland through Waterford. Upon the news that the larger Irish army was defeated by a Dublin garrison led by Michael Jones at Rathmines, Cromwell went to Dublin instead of Waterford. His campaign saw Wexford surrender, before attempting to capture Duncannon, which was seen to be of integral strategic importance to the defence of Waterford. Eventually they had to change tack and approach Waterford from Carrick-on-Suir, which allowed Cromwell to cross the Suir and set up camp at Kilbarry. Approaching the city walls, Cromwell was met by fire from the Waterford trainbands. He met the city's mayor, John Levitt, who asked for fifteen days to consider whether Waterford should surrender. In the meantime, Levitt had secured two regiments totalling 1,500 men from Ormond while Cromwell moved his camp to the south-east of the city. Artillery arrived from New Ross at Great Island and it appeared that Cromwell's forces would finally overpower the besieged city. However, the weather would play a part. Torrential rain led to many of Cromwell's men falling ill, which left him with the only option of having to end the siege of Waterford due to lack of manpower. Waterford was the only city not to fall to the efforts of Cromwell. It did eventually surrender in August 1650 to Cromwell's son-in-law, General Ireton.

During the 1640s, a number of privateering groups came into operation, with around fifty in the Waterford/Wexford area. These privateers would sell their captured spoils of fish, beef, pork, wine and oil, to name a few such items, and one commentator observed that the 'cellars and storehouses at Waterford are full of Englishmen's goods, and the Irish there come and trade for them familiarly'. By the end of the decade, Waterford was the only county where a surplus of grain could be found in Ireland.

However, after Cromwell's campaign in Ireland, towns where Catholics had been in positions of authority such as Waterford went into decline as a result of the fall of Catholic economic influence.

It was planned that Waterford would become an entirely Protestant enclave as part of the Restoration development of the Cromwellian settlement of Ireland. The plan collapsed but was part of the development of Protestant settlers staying within the confines of the city walls while Catholics were largely to be found outside the city's defences.

WATERFORD AND THE JACOBITE WAR, 1688–91

Upon James II being crowned king in 1685, the corporation of Waterford City sent a note of loyalty to the new monarch. The Protestant-dominated council began to admit Catholics as freemen, such as John Donoghue, James Lynch, Henry Keating, Paul Sherlock and Martin Welch in July 1686.

The process of dissolving such assemblies began under the Earl of Tyrconnell with Waterford Corporation disbanded and replaced with a Catholic majority council with Richard Fitzgerald as mayor. When James was deposed by his son-in-law, William of Orange, Tyrconnell tried to raise an army to help his mother to take control of the throne. A 400-man regiment raised by the Earl of Tyrone, Richard Power, was billeted at Waterford in 1689. The same year, James came to Ireland and held Parliament, which outlawed and sought to confiscate the land of Protestants who supported William.

The Siege of Derry saw 'Roche the Swimmer' swim 3 miles up the River Foyle to inform the citizens of the city that Kirke's relief ships were near. Roche was granted the Waterford estate of James Everard and ferry rights which included that of crossing the River Suir at Waterford. These ferry rights were eventually bought outright by Waterford Corporation in 1907 for the sum of £63,000.

After the Battle of the Boyne, James fled to Waterford with the mortally wounded Sir Neal O'Neill whose tomb can be seen in French Church in the city. He would eventually reach France, while William sent cavalry forces to Waterford from Carrick-on-Suir on 21 July.

The Jacobite garrison at Waterford numbered 1,500 infantry but both parties entered into negotiations. The city was given three days to make a decision on accepting terms outlined by the Williamite forces. Gentle persuasion was provided by William, who sent five regiments of foot soldiers under General Kirke towards the city. On the fourth day, terms were accepted and William reached the defences of Waterford by 25 June 1690. However, he did not enter the city but ordered that the citizens of Waterford were not to be distressed and took 1000 tons of French flour from the city's reserves.

The city would become an important port for supplies for Williamite forces after Duncannon Fort came under their control. The Protestant Corporation was restored, with David Lloyd becoming Mayor of Waterford. William would return to England via Waterford. His Secretary of State, Sir Robert Southwell, noted of his departure journey from Ireland that 'on the first of September his majesty came from Carrick To Waterford and had a fair view of that city. The river was filled with trading ships, who all fired their guns and gave great acclamations as he passed.'

A Danish contingent of the Williamite army was based at Waterford during the winter of 1690–91 under the Duke of Wurtemburg. However, they had not received payment from William and began to threaten plundering the urban areas of Ireland such as warning of the ransacking of Waterford. The corporation of the city passed a payment of £144 to the duke to avoid the threat being carried out.

The result of Waterford surrendering meant that the citizens of the city were pardoned by William in 1693.

THE QUAKERS IN WATERFORD

The introduction of the Act for Encouraging Protestant Strangers in Ireland in 1662 saw an acceleration in groups such as Huguenots and Quakers coming and settling in Ireland. Yet prior to this there was a Dutch Catholic community in Waterford. The Quakers' presence in Ireland dates to 1654 and would form an important part in the commercial and industrial affairs of Waterford City.

Parva Roma – Little Rome: Waterford in the Sixteenth and Seventeenth Centuries

The Quakers in Waterford based themselves in the parish of St John from 1655. They acquired a meeting house just off Bowling Green Lane (where the Christian Brothers School on Manor Street was later located) in 1694. This site was a burial ground in the seventeenth and nineteenth centuries and was later assumed by Waterford Corporation in 1950 and developed into Wyse Park. These lands previously belonged to William Wyse, who was given them upon the dissolution of the monasteries by Henry VIII, and were later acquired by the Quakers.

In 1798, the Quakers founded Newtown School which continues with its ethos to this day. It was built on the estate which had been the home of Sir Thomas Wyse, a noted figure in the history of Irish education. The school was founded by charter for the Quaker population of the province of Munster. Initially, the main house was used for boarding, with a stable converted into classrooms. In 1813, there was the addition of a library. Further developments included the infirmary and lecture hall, swimming pool in 1890, gymnasium in 1892 and reputedly the first school laboratory in Ireland in 1895. The school was close to closing in 1925 but under the stewardship of Arnold Marsh saw increased numbers, and the school thriving. The school now boasts all-weather hockey pitches, an outdoor swimming pool added in the early 1970s, and the William Glynn Science Building in 1977.

The Quaker community provided relief in the city during the famine in the 1840s with the Tuskar Lodging House and Munster Dining Rooms. Around 1893, the meeting house moved to O'Connell Street (where Garter Lane is today) and finally settling at Newtown in 1973.

Significant Quaker families in the business sphere in the nineteenth century included the Malcolmsons, with their cotton mill at Portlaw and Neptune shipbuilding company at Adelphi Quay. One of their ships was the SS *Una* which was the first ship to journey through the Suez Canal. The Penroses and Whites also had substantial interests in shipping. Brewing in Waterford was dominated by Quakers such as Davis, Goffs and Strangmans. The Penrose name would become synonymous with glass-making in the city, while Jacobs established their first biscuit-making factory at 33 Bridge Street in Waterford City.

In 2014, a memorial at the site of the first Quaker burial ground was unveiled at John's Lane. There is an angled wall which bears the family names of those interred in the graveyard.

5

THE CRYSTAL CITY:
Eighteenth-Century Waterford

TIMELINE

1703 CE: Waterford City has a piped water supply from this date.

1704 CE: Waterford Corporation lifts limitations on Catholics trading in the city.

1710 CE: For the first time, Catholics are admitted as freemen of the City of Waterford.

1727 CE: St Patrick's Church is built on Patrick's Street.

1732 CE: Street lighting is installed at the main streets in the city.

1733 CE: The Bishop of Waterford and Lismore, Thomas Miles, has St Olaf's Church rebuilt at his own expense.

1736 CE: Waterford Corporation commission the Dutch artist Van der Hagen to paint the Waterford Quayside. It is one of the earliest paintings of a view of an Irish city.

1744 CE: Food riots in Waterford City.

1746 CE: Charles Smith's *History of Waterford* is published.

1773 CE: Waterford Corporation resolves for Christ Church to be rebuilt.

1783 CE: George and William Penrose establish Waterford Glass.

1784 CE: The Leper Hospital is built on John's Hill. It's later known as the City and County Infirmary from 1897.

1788 CE: The Town Hall is constructed.

1792 CE: Waterford Corporation is petitioned for a site to be granted for the building of a Roman Catholic cathedral. The corporation grant the request with a lease of 999 years for a yearly rent of 2 shillings and 6 pence. Construction started the following year but it would take nearly 130 years before it is consecrated. It was completed in 1796 at Barronstrand Street at a cost of £20,000.

1793 CE: The construction of Waterford's first bridge spanning the River Suir starts on 30 April 1793 costing £14,000. It would be colloquially known as 'Timbertoes' because of its wooden form and forty sets of piers. It was 42ft in breadth and 832ft in length, and opened in January 1794.

1798 CE: The first school in Waterford City is established by the Presentation Sisters at Jenkins Lane.

1799 CE: The first Fever Hospital in Ireland is built at John's Hill in Waterford.

The quay of this city, which is above half a mile in length and of considerable breadth, is not inferior to, but rather exceeds the most celebrated in Europe ... The Exchange, Customhouse and other public buildings, besides the houses of the merchants and the citizens, ranged along the quay are no small addition to its beauty ... The whole is fronted with hewn stone, well paved and in some places forty foot broad.

Dr Charles Smith, 1746

The spirit of industry and commerce seems to me to be more active at Waterford than in any other Irish town, more active even than at Cork, although the size of the town is much less.

De Latocnaye, from *A Frenchman's Walk Through Ireland*, 1796–97

WATERFORD:
Transformation from Medieval Enclave to a Modern European City

In the eighteenth century the city of Waterford was transformed from a medieval walled settlement to a modern European city. The medieval city defences were removed in sections, while churches from the same period were modified to follow contemporary architectural trends. The city expanded with the diverting of St John's River and the creation of a new suburb called Newtown. Today nearly 90 per cent of the buildings of architectural or historic interest date to either the twelfth, thirteenth or eighteenth centuries. The 1690s saw the process of demolishing parts of the city walls, with the removal of gates beginning in 1695. The wall which ran along the quayside was knocked down and the artillery blockhouse by Reginald's Tower destroyed in 1711. After the alterations to the city's defences, six towers remain completely intact to this day.

The process of building three- and four-storey red-brick houses in the 'Dutch Billy' style along the Quay was the next major development as the appearance of Waterford was drastically altered. The suburb of Ballybricken was linked to the quays with the making of King's Street (now part of modern-day O'Connell Street), Hanover Street and New Road (present-day Thomas Street), which were completed by 1764. Furthermore, the choice of street names were reflections of the Protestant Corporation who administered the city and sought to illustrate Waterford's continued faithfulness to the English crown.

The Dublin Parliament was governed by a Protestant Ascendancy with the Penal Laws (to limit political and economic undertakings) placing restrictions on Catholics. This led to many Catholic families from Waterford migrating to continental Europe, such as France and Spain. Those who remained in the city were not allowed to hold public office, though some were made freemen of Waterford. Religious affiliation among the inhabitants of the city included Baptists, Presbyterians and Quakers by the middle of the eighteenth century. A new period of affluence saw street lights erected in Waterford in 1732, and the creation of the Mall where St John's River once flowed took place in the same decade. In 1746, the historian Charles Smith pronounced the Mall:

> a beautiful walk, about 200 yards long and proportionably broad … it is planted with rows of Elms, and the sides of the walks are fenced with a stone wall … Here the Ladies and Gentlemen assemble on fine evenings where they have the opportunity of each other's conversation. Nothing

can be more agreeable than to see this shady walk crowded with the fair sex of the City, taking the air, enjoying the charms of a pleasant evening, and improving their healths …

The prosperity the city enjoyed in the eighteenth century saw the corporation commission the artist William Van Der Hagen to paint the *View of Waterford* in 1736 for the sum of £20.

In eighteenth-century Ireland, Waterford was the third-best-connected port, trading with over 400 ports from Britain to mainland Europe and North America to Scandinavia, with goods exported being butter, pork and salted beef. One of the important trade routes was to Newfoundland, with seasonal trade in the cod fishing industry leading to around 33,000 people migrating from the Irish city to that area in Canada well into the opening decades of the nineteenth century. Fifty ships were based in the port of Waterford by 1770, many owned by Catholic merchants.

The 1700s also saw the construction of the Bishop's Palace and refurbishment of Christ Church Cathedral in Waterford. The latter part of the century saw a development in relations between Catholics and Protestants, with the Catholic Relief Act of 1793 allowing Catholics to have the same voting rights as Protestants for parliamentary elections, though Catholics could still not become members of parliament. Waterford can assert that it was the first place in the British Isles where a Catholic cathedral was built after the Reformation. The architect John Roberts, a Protestant, has the distinction of being the only man to design both the Catholic and Protestant cathedrals in the same city in northern Europe. Roberts's legacy can still be seen today as many of the important civic buildings in Waterford are of his design. The architectural historian Edward McParland has noted that:

Waterford more than any other city in the country in the late 18th century succeeded in expressing its civic dignity with fitting architectural grandeur … The density and quality of building in Waterford, however, made the city architecturally pre-eminent. No city of its size had, within its boundaries, as grand a bishop's palace. No 18th-century cathedral elsewhere in the country – with the possible exception of Cashel – outdid either of John Robert's two Waterford cathedrals.

The Wide Streets Commission saw the widening of Barronstrand Street, and the elimination of Little Barronstrand Street, Garter Lane and Royal Oak Lane to create an open area north of Broad Street by 1784. The formation of the Apple Market by John Street was aided by the demolition of a block of buildings which originally stood in the area. The first bridge across the River Suir was a great addition to the infrastructure of the city in 1794. It was built by the American Lemuel Cox at the cost of £14,000. Locally it was known as Timbertoes, and the wooden bridge remained in existence until 1913 when it was replaced by John Redmond Bridge.

One of the notable industries that started in the city was a glass factory established by brothers George and William Penrose in 1783, which existed until 1851. The Penrose family were Quakers, a religious community which made up to 2 per cent of Waterford's population. They created the chandeliers which adorn the interior of City Hall and the earliest piece still in existence from this factory is a wine decanter dating to 1789, now housed in the Bishop's Palace Museum.

THOMAS 'BULLOCKS' WYSE:
Eccentric Catholic Merchant

Thomas Wyse, born in 1701, was a successful industrialist who reopened the copper mines in Bunmahon, County Waterford in 1750. He married Elizabeth Bourne and together they had six children. Wyse lived in France where two of his sons served in the Irish Brigade of the French army.

He was nicknamed 'Bullocks' for his use of bullocks to draw his carriage instead of horses in protest against the Penal Laws, which stipulated that a Catholic would have to accept an offer of £5 from a Protestant for a horse. The same laws meant Wyse as a Catholic could not take part in the political affairs of the city.

In 1756, Wyse was involved in the creation of the Catholic Committee, the first organisation to stand for the business interests of the Catholic community. He proposed a subscription to fund the organisation but this was impeded by the bishops. One could argue it was a forerunner for Daniel O'Connell's rent repeal in the nineteenth century. Easily roused, Wyse had his men remove one of the gates of the city's defences, as it limited access to his estate.

Of his industrial interests in the city and county of Waterford, Wyse noted in 1770, 'I have laid out a considerable part of my annual income these twenty years past and upwards to introduce sundry manufactures not before attempted in this kingdom.' This included the founding of a copper smelter near the city in 1747 which expanded to comprise granaries, bakehouse and windmill. Though there was one failure in the following decade, when a hardware factory he established was unsuccessful.

'Bullocks' Wyse died in 1770. He had three sons, one of whom, Richard, followed the Protestant faith. His son John inherited that lands at Newtown and commissioned John Roberts to design Newtown House, which later became Newtown School, established by the Quaker community in the city. His eldest son Francis would go on to inherit the entire estate upon the death of his two brothers. Thomas 'Bullocks' Wyse's grandson, Sir Thomas Wyse (son of Francis), is explored later in this study.

JOHN ROBERTS:
Architect of Georgian Waterford

A son of an architect and builder, John Roberts was born in Waterford City in 1712. His mother died young, leaving him and his three sisters in the care of his father. He received most of his architectural training in London and is believed to have returned to his hometown around 1744. He married Mary Susannah Sautelle, a daughter of a wealthy French officer; the pair eloped and Mary was disinherited by her father. They lived on Patrick Street for a time.

In 1746, Roberts was tasked with completing the works on the Bishop's Palace by Bishop Richard Chenevix. The cleric, happy with the Waterford architect's work, commissioned him to build some houses and leased him the old palace on Cathedral Square. It was at this location that the Roberts family lived for the next fifty years.

Other projects designed in the city by Roberts include the Leper Hospital in 1785, Newtown House in 1786 (which later became Newtown School), City Hall in 1788 and the residence of William Morris in 1795 which became the Chamber of Commerce. It houses a remarkable spiral staircase.

Roberts was nicknamed 'Honest John' for the way he treated his workers by paying them on Saturday mornings so they could purchase the best produce that the weekend markets had to offer. He even gave half of his workers' wages to their wives, so it would not be all spent in public houses.

His two most significant works in Waterford City are the Protestant and Catholic cathedrals, which are explored in more detail later in this study. The latter of these is notable as being the first Catholic cathedral built in post-Reformation Ireland. However, Roberts would not see the project completed, with the legend of his death being that he awoke one morning at three o'clock and went to the construction site where none of the workers was present. He then fell asleep on the ground which led to pneumonia, and died on 23 May 1796.

Roberts is said to have had between twenty-one and twenty-four children, with only eight surviving to adulthood. Two of his sons, Thomas Roberts and Thomas Sautelle Roberts, were landscape painters. Notable descendants include his grandson Sir Abraham Roberts, a general in the Indian army and colonel of the Bengal Fusiliers, and his great-grandson Field-Marshal Lord Roberts, commander-in-chief of the British army.

VAN DER HAGEN'S *VIEW OF WATERFORD*, 1736

The landscape painting of Waterford City by William Van der Hagen was commissioned by Waterford Corporation in 1736 for the amount of £20. Frank Heylin notes that the task of the artist was 'to portray our city "warts and all". The picture is somewhat idealised, but enables us to form a rather good idea of the Waterford of that day.' Van der Hagen is considered the father of Irish landscape painting and another of his works related to the city is an altarpiece in St Patrick's Church.

In the painting one can see the expanse of the Quay, thirty years after the demolition of the city's medieval defences along it. Reginald's Tower is still prominent, while the city wall is replaced by 'Dutch Billies' that are lined along the Quay.

To the west of the city, we can see medieval towers and the remains of the city walls as well as the bell towers of Blackfriars, Christ Church Cathedral

Van der Hagen's *View of Waterford*, 1736. The first oil-painted landscape of the city and a statement of the prosperity which Waterford enjoyed at that time. *Courtesy of Waterford Treasures*

(before it was redeveloped as the Georgian edifice designed by John Roberts) and Greyfriars. Also present is the floodplain of St John's River – the Pill.

In the foreground, hay is being hoarded to the left, in the middle cattle are grazing, while the gentry are rambling in the scene. The landscape is as much a statement of the Protestant hegemony which governed the city as it is a declaration of the prosperity of Waterford at this time.

The Exchange housed the painting until the City Hall was built.

THE MALL

The Mall, meaning promenade or walkway, was developed in the eighteenth century, extending from Reginald's Tower to Colbeck Street. The area was known as Miller's Marsh and was the location of Colbeck's Mill and mill pond, the latter of which covered a large part of what makes up the Mall today. The mill was located south-east of Reginald's Tower, with an early reference dating to *c.* 1224 noting it as the 'Mill of Caldebac'. Subsequently, the mill came into the possession of the Knights Templar and was leased to Walter le Devneys in 1326. It came into the ownership of William Wyse after the dissolution and suppression of monasteries in 1540 by Henry VIII.

The corporation considered developing a bowling green and walking area in the early eighteenth century. Located at Rose Lane on the northern section of the Mall, the Bowling Green, for members only, was launched in 1735. In 1737, the development of the Mall began (referred to as the 'Old Mall') and was lined with elm trees on either side of the street. The Assembly Rooms and playhouse were built on the Mall by 1788. An early civic event held in the Assembly Rooms was a breakfast for Prince William Henry, the future King William IV.

Lord William Beresford's funeral cortege along the Mall on 3 January 1901. Beresford was a recipient of the Victoria Cross for his efforts in the Anglo-Zulu War. He reached the rank of Lieutenant-Colonel and is buried at Clonagem Churchyard in County Waterford. *Poole Collection, WP 1160, National Library of Ireland*

Boys' Brigade off to New Ross, Sunday, 28 May 1898. City Hall on the Mall can be seen in the background. *Poole Collection, IMP 563, National Library of Ireland*

The year 1816 saw the corporation move from the Exchange on the Quay to the Assembly Rooms to hold council meetings, leading to the building becoming the Town Hall.

OLD WATERFORD NEWSPAPERS

The first local paper to be noted was the *Waterford Flying Post*, which was in existence in 1729 and printed locally. This was followed by the *Waterford Journal* in 1765, which ran for six years. In the same year as the *Journal*, *Ramsey's Waterford Chronicle* was established, which subsequently became the *Waterford Chronicle*, which ceased in 1910.

The *Waterford Mirror and Munster Packet* was founded in 1801 and became known as the *Waterford Mirror,* which ran until 1910. The *Munster Packet* had existed since 1788 and was incorporated into the *Mirror.*

The *Waterford Herald* which operated from 1791 to 1795 was noted by J.S. Carroll as 'little more than a mouthpiece for the Government of the day'. Around the same time as the *Herald,* there was *Carey's Waterford Packet,* which did not last long.

The Conservative paper, the *Waterford Mail,* existed from 1823 until 1908, and the more Liberal-inclined *Waterford News* started in 1848. There was also the *Waterford Citizen,* which ran from 1859 to 1906.

Local papers that are little known include the *Celt, Waterford Spectator, Waterford Advertiser* and the *Waterford Evening Telegraph.*

By the start of the twentieth century, papers in existence in Waterford included the *Waterford Chronicle, Waterford Mirror, Waterford Daily Mail, Waterford News-Letter, Waterford News, Evening News, Munster Express, Waterford Standard,* and *Waterford Star.*

BISHOP'S PALACE

The site of the Bishop's Palace has been a residence for the Bishop of Waterford since 1096 when the city was granted its first prelate. The original drawings for the Georgian palace were by Richard Castle in 1743, but the project was never started. The job was given to John R1oberts to oversee.

The year 1820 saw the head gardener of the grounds of the Bishop's Palace, Richard Darcy, and his wife murdered by James Darcy, Richard's brother. They were poisoned with arsenic by James who stood to inherit their savings. The plot was uncovered by Dr Thomas Lewis Mackesy, who interviewed all members of staff of the palace and discovered the remainder of the poison. James Darcy was hanged for his crime.

The palace was the residence of the Church of Ireland Bishop of Waterford and Lismore until the early twentieth century. It has since been a school and council offices. The Bishop's Palace is now a museum covering the history of the city from the eighteenth to the twentieth century.

Above left: Bishop's Palace, the Mall, Waterford City. *Courtesy of Waterford Treasures*

Above right: Mrs Jordan in the character of Hypolita, 1791 (photographic reproduction). Jordan was an Anglo-Irish actress and mistress to the future King William VI of the United Kingdom. She would have ten children with the Duke of Clarence before he became monarch.

NOTABLE PERSONALITIES OF GEORGIAN WATERFORD

The actress Dorothy Jordan was born Dorothy Bland in Waterford on 22 November 1761. In 1777, she made her stage debut in Dublin as Phoebe in Shakespeare's *As You Like It*. Two years later she performed in the Henry Fielding farce *The Virgin Unmasked* at the Crow Street Theatre in Dublin. Jordan joined the regional troop of Tate Wilkinson until 1785 before treading the boards in London. She retired from acting in 1814. Jordan gave birth to a daughter to her first manager in Dublin, three children to Richard Ford and ten children to the Duke of Clarence, who later became King William IV. The children of the Duke bore the name FitzClarence, and the eldest was made the Earl of Munster. The Duke and Jordan separated in 1811. She moved to France in 1815 and died a year later. Jordan was the subject of portraits by Sir Joshua Reynolds and Thomas Gainsborough.

The novelist Regina Roche (née Dalton) was born in Waterford in 1764. She wrote over fifteen works of romantic and Gothic fiction, with her most well-known work being *Children of the Abbey* published in 1796.

Former editor of the *Times* (London) Edward Sterling was born in Waterford in 1773. As a young man he joined the Yeomanry and fought on the English side against the insurgents of the 1798 rebellion in Ireland (fighting at Vinegar Hill). He became a member of staff at the *Times* then later was made editor of the paper, gaining the nickname 'The Thunderer'. Sterling died in 1847.

CITY HALL

The Town Hall is the centre of the civic administration of the city ... and is one of the most imposing buildings on the Mall.

Irish Trade Union Congress, Waterford, August 1939: Souvenir and Guide

The Mayors' Treasury in the foyer of City Hall details the history of the governance of the city from the Vikings to the creation of the Mayoralty in 1272 and into the twenty-first century. *Courtesy of Waterford Treasures*

Originally the Assembly Rooms, designed by John Roberts for the wealthy merchant classes to frequent, the construction of what is now the City Hall began in 1783. On 4 August 1785, the first ball staged in the Assembly Rooms was held. Later it was decided that the mayor of the city would have the use of the first floor for public events. The two-storey building comprises a committee room, council chambers and a large room for civic engagements. The latter was completed in 1788, originally to function as a ballroom, which explains the gallery in the room which would have been used by orchestras. Well-known figures to have spoken in the Large Room include Irish nationalists such as Daniel O'Connell, Charles Stewart Parnell, Patrick Pearse and the American abolitionist Frederick Douglas.

The Council Room is decorated with a cut-glass chandelier produced by Waterford Glass. A copy of the chandelier is in the Hall of Independence in Philadelphia in the United States. During the 1798 Rebellion, the North Cork Militia was accommodated at the Assembly Rooms.

An exhibition titled 'The Mayors' Treasury' is housed in City Hall and illustrates the civic governance of Waterford, from the city's first recorded mayor Roger le Lom in 1284 to the twenty-first-century office-holders, with twenty-three objects dating from 1080 to the present day.

THEATRE ROYAL

'[i]n serving our Irish theatre we endeavour to preserve the spirit of art and liberty for all our citizens. That is why it is our privilege to be called on to re-open the Theatre Royal as a national provincial centre of drama with the premiere of a play concerned with the spirit of liberty.'

Cyril Cusack, speaking on the night the Theatre Royal was re-opened in March 1958, performing a play about Roger Casement.

The Theatre Royal is Ireland's oldest theatre in continuous operation. It is a Victorian horseshoe theatre inside a Georgian building. The theatre opened in 1785 and the first play to be staged there was Shakespeare's *As You Like It*. The Theatre Royal was host to many renowned performers of eighteenth-century theatre, such as the 'Swedish Nightingale' Jenny Lind and the Limerick-born prima donna of La Scala in Milan, Catherine Hayes.

The Waterford-born Shakespearean actor Charles Keane performed at the theatre in 1836. The building was converted to the auditorium that exists today in 1876. The night the theatre re-opened it was not able to cope adequately with the large crowd that had gathered. The police were needed to bring some semblance of control as some women fainted and a crush began. *John Royston's Comedy and Opera Bouffe* was the first act to perform in the new Theatre Royal. In 1882, smoking was prohibited within the theatre, with a £2 fine the penalty if caught in the act. Those who behaved in a 'foul or filthy manner' were subject to a £5 charge.

The theatre primarily staged musicals until 1906. Two significant performers to have played the Theatre Royal were Percy French and John McCormack. The theatre was leased to John Collins in 1910 for cinematograph performances. This was followed by Lawrence and Martin Breen running the Theatre Royal as both a cinema and theatre. The Buffalo Bill Cody Show played the theatre, where it is purported that they shot the lights out for the finale of the performance.

By 1955, the theatre had fallen into financial difficulties and was considered unsustainable by the corporation. In response to this, the Theatre Royal Society was formed in 1956 to try to save the theatre from closure. March 1958 saw the theatre re-open with a play about Irish nationalist Roger Casement with Cyril Cusack performing the lead role.

Deemed to be the 'people's theatre', since re-opening in the 1950s it has played host to the Festival of Light Opera, Féile na Scoileanna, Tops of the Town and the Waterford Pantomime Society. The Nobel prize-winning playwright Harold Pinter and Waterford-born Tony Award-winning actress Anna Manahan have both performed on the stage of the Theatre Royal.

The director of the theatre, Ben Barnes, oversaw extensive renovations of the theatre which were completed by 2009. It re-opened with the performance of a Bernard Farrell play titled *Wallace, Balfe and Mr Bunn*. In 2014, to coincide with the 1,100th anniversary of the founding of Waterford, the opera *The Invader*, composed by Eric Sweeney and Mark Roper, was performed.

The Penrose Decanter is the oldest piece of Waterford glass still in existence. The historian John M. Hearne notes of the object that it has a 'noticeably wide pouring lip as is common to most Penrose decanters'.

OLDEST SURVIVING PIECE OF WATERFORD GLASS

The Penrose decanter made in 1789 has a wide pouring lip and a three-ring neck. On the base the words 'Penrose Waterford' are moulded. The decanter is lavishly swollen in the body with high comb flutes. There is prismatic cutting on the shoulder. The cut of the glass is by pendant semi-circle arches which are lined with fine diamond with trefoil splits among the arches.

CATHOLIC CATHEDRAL OF THE MOST HOLY TRINITY

A very large Roman Catholic Chapel, or Cathedral, in this town. A light gallery affords the only fixed seats a remarkable feature in the Roman Catholic places of worship; and in which they have a great advantage over the Protestants, as to the true object of such buildings: all are open, and open alike to rich and poor: no appropriation of seats, or locked pews, or passport of money required. In this respect more appearance at least of devotion and spiritual service.

James Glassford, *Three Tours in Ireland*, 1824–26 (1832)

Ireland's oldest Catholic cathedral was designed by the architect John Roberts and built in 1793. The initial T-shaped church was expanded in 1829 with a chancel added to the east and subsequently renovated in 1854. In the 1890s an Ionic limestone frontispiece was added. The interior of the cathedral is a tiled floor, with Corinthian columns, carved timber pews and a timber-panelled gallery to the first floor. There are ten Waterford Crystal chandeliers which

West front of the Holy Trinity Cathedral of the Roman Catholic diocese of Waterford and Lismore (Merlante). It is Ireland's oldest Roman Catholic cathedral and the first to be built in Ireland after the Reformation.

were gifted by the producer to the cathedral. The stained-glass windows of the cathedral were produced by Mayer and Co. of Munich in 1885. The current organ situated in the church was built by William Hill and Sons of Liverpool in the 1850s, costing £1,700 at the time. The organ was first played by W.T. Best on 29 August 1858. The cathedral was refurbished in 1977 after the Second Vatican Council with a new altar fitted to face the congregation. The latest renovation of the Catholic cathedral took place in 2006.

SIR THOMAS WYSE (1791–1862):
Politician and Educational Reformer

Born in Waterford on 24 December 1791, Sir Thomas Wyse was educated at a Jesuit college named Stonyhurst in England, and subsequently attended Trinity College, Dublin from 1808 to 1812. His 'Grand Tour of Europe' would see him become acquainted with Letitia Bonaparte (niece of Napoleon Bonaparte) whom he would marry in 1821. They would have two children, though they would separate near the end of the 1820s.

Catholic Emancipation was achieved by the time Wyse was elected MP for Tipperary. In parliament, his main interest was educational reform. He would advocate multi-denominational education with specific religious instruction provided on another day, and the creation of provincial colleges to provide university instruction and education. Wyse's proposals would presage the 'national system' of Irish education and the Queen's Colleges Act of 1845.

In 1832, Wyse competed for the seat of Waterford City, only to be defeated, and then subsequently elected for the same constituency in 1834.

He was appointed as a lord of the treasury in the Melbourne government in 1839, becoming one of the first Catholics to be a member of the British government after Catholic Emancipation of ten years previous. In addition, he chaired committees on English legal education and the endorsement of fine arts. However, he would lose his seat in Waterford in 1847.

Wyse was made a British ambassador to Greece in 1849, which would see him involved in the Don Pacifico incident (an attack on the Portuguese consul's house) and the development of the Crimean War. In 1857, Wyse was knighted, and returned to Greece to deal with financial reform of the Greek state, while also advocating reform of the Greek legal and penal systems. He died in Athens on 15 April 1862.

WILLIAM HOBSON:
First Governor of New Zealand

William Hobson was born in Waterford in 1793. In 1803, he joined the Royal Navy and served during the Napoleonic wars and in the suppression of piracy in the Caribbean. Promoted to the position of commander in 1824, Hobson went on to serve in the Indian and Pacific Oceans.

In 1837, Hobson sailed to New Zealand upon the request of a British resident, James Busby, who felt endangered by wars involving Maori tribes. Three years later he returned to New Zealand as its first governor. Hobson died on 10 September 1842. His remains are interred at Symons Street Cemetery in Auckland.

TIMBERTOES:
the Waterford Bridge, 1793–1911

The visitor who arrives at Waterford by rail has to cross the bridge to get into the city. Strange as it may seem there was no bridge over the river at Waterford until the old wooden bridge was completed by 1794 …

Irish Trade Union Congress, Waterford, August 1939: Souvenir and Guide

River Suir, *c.* 1890 to *c.* 1900. Timbertoes, designed by Lemuel Cox, was deemed a huge task as the River Suir is five times wider and much deeper than the Liffey in Dublin. *Library of Congress*

The wooden bridge was designed by the American Lemuel Cox and was 832ft in length. This was later reduced to 734ft due to extensions to the quays at either end of the bridge. Originally a toll bridge, after time a demand rose for the bridge to be free of any charge for crossing it. The timber bridge, which was made up of forty sets of oaken piers, was modified to have a drawbridge at the middle later. It cost £14,000 to build in 1794.

A severe cold spell with frost and ice freezing the River Suir in January 1881, which threatened the existence of the bridge. The decision was taken by the Bridge Commissioners for dynamite to be used to explode the ice by an Edward Jacob. This operation failed, which lead to the deployment of a steam tug to create a semi-circle by the central part of the bridge, thus taking the strain off the arches. Eventually the ice receded (dispersed by each tide) and it was resolved by committee that two steam tugs, the *Father Matthew* and the *Suir*, be used until the end of the month.

It was decided in 1900 by the Privy Council that the wooden bridge, over 100 years old, would be replaced with a ferro-concrete bridge using the Hennibique system. Finally, in 1907, Waterford Corporation acquired the bridge for the sum of £63,000.

Construction of the new bridge began in 1910 and it was opened in February 1913, being 700ft in length. It was later named the John Redmond Bridge in honour of the MP for the city who opened the bridge.

PHILIP LONG: IRISH REBEL

From a Catholic family, born during the 1770s, it is believed Long may have lived in Spain from the late 1780s to 1795. He was an important financial backer of the 1803 Rebellion led by Robert Emmet. His wealth resulted from a partnership with his uncle, John Roche, who was a merchant. At Rouen in France, he financed a cotton mill which provided the cover to organise the insurrection. Prior to this, he was involved in publishing the 'Military regulations of the council of war' for Emmet though did not raise any suspicions from Dublin Castle.

At his residence at 4 Crow Street in Dublin, many meetings were held to plan the rebellion. In total, it would cost £1,400 for arms and materials. Long was arrested in August when documents connecting him with the plan were found in his home. He composed an address to the 'Citizens of Dublin' which was far more provocative than Emmet's proclamation, urging them to take to arms against their oppressors. While imprisoned, he distanced himself from the failed rebellion and was eventually released in 1806. He had been deemed a key conspirator in order to receive new charges related to it. During his time in jail his health and wealth had declined considerably. He operated as a wine merchant until 1809 and died unmarried in 1814.

BARRACK STREET

Barrack Street was so called after the military barracks which were established in the area in the late eighteenth and early nineteenth centuries, the first of which was the Infantry Barrack built on the Barley Fields which is now on the north side of Barrack Street. The corporation leased the land to the military with construction on the barrack starting in 1798. The Artillery Barrack (built in 1805) was located at the south-west end of the street and was leased by Thomas Wyse of the Manor of St John to the military for a tenure of 999 years from 25 March 1805.

In the seventeenth century, the area formed part of a common green and became part of the road system of the city connected to Newgate. It is referred to as the 'Great Road' from the city to Kilbarry in 1717. The area became known as the Faha from the eighteenth century.

There was a small maternity or lying-in hospital established in 1834 opposite the Infantry Barrack (which was moved to Parliament Street four years later).

The Infantry Barrack became the lone Garda Station in Waterford City in 1930 upon the closure of three other stations in the city, and would remain there for ten years.

6

WATERFORD IN THE LONG NINETEENTH CENTURY

TIMELINE

1802 CE: At New Street, Edmund Rice establishes his first school while construction commences of Mount Sion. On 1 May 1804, Bishop John Power blesses the grounds of Mount Sion.

1812 CE: The composer William Vincent Wallace is born in Colbeck Street in the city.

1816 CE: The Ursuline Convent is founded in Waterford.

1818 CE: The *Waterford Mirror* asserts on 18 October that it is the first newspaper in Ireland to be printed by gaslight.

1819 CE: On 17 May, food riots occur in Waterford City.

1820 CE: Henry Denny establishes his first bacon factory at Bridge Street (then known as Queen Street).

1823 CE: The birth of Thomas Francis Meagher at the Granville Hotel on 3 August.

1824 CE: Ryland's *History, Topography and Antiquities of the County and City of Waterford* is published.

1826 CE: The Bank of Ireland opens in Waterford on 6 March.

1829 CE: On 2 January, the Quay is the first street in Waterford lit by gaslight.

1832 CE: There is an outbreak of cholera in Waterford City leading to 192 deaths over three months.

1841 CE: The Waterford Union Workhouse opens on 15 March.

1842 CE: The Fanning Institute opens on 25 October on the grounds previously belonging to the House of Industry. In the same year, the Catholic University opens at St Stephen Street on 24 September.

1846 CE: The SS *Neptune*, built by the Neptune shipyard, is launched and goes on to be used in the London–St Petersburg route.

1848 CE: Ballinaneashagh Cemetery opens on 15 March.

1849 CE: On 12 July, the Court House opens, built on the site of St Catherine's Abbey. It is designed by the architect John B. Keane.

1850 CE: On 1 November, a Tenants Rights meeting is held at Ballybricken.

1850 CE: Six hundred emigrants sail from Waterford Quay for America on 16 May. By December of the year, 20,000 people had emigrated from New Ross and Waterford since 1846.

1853 CE: The first train from Waterford to Tramore operates on 5 September.

1857 CE: The Royal Agricultural Show is held at the People's Park in Waterford City. A bridge connecting the park and the Court House is named in honour of the Lord Lieutenant Lord Carlisle who attends the event. In November of 1857, the park is handed over to the citizens of Waterford, with the first Park Ranger being Alderman W. Johnson.

1861 CE: The Clock Tower is built in the Quay at a cost of £150. It is designed by Mr Tarrant and is located on the site of an old fish market. Also, a clock is erected at the Applemarket around this time.

1864 CE: On 14 April, the last public execution is held at Ballybricken Jail.

1867 CE: In January, the River Suir freezes, with floating icebergs nearly causing damage to the bridge.

1869 CE: The lower parts of Waterford City are flooded, leading to people having to leave their homes, while the People's Park resembles a lake.

1873 CE: Bishop Power lays the foundation stone for the Little Sisters of the Poor Convent at Manor Hill on 13 July. Earlier in February of that year, there is a heavy snow fall measuring up to 4ft in the city.

1874 CE: The foundation stone for the Dominican Church on Bridge Street is laid.

1875 CE: The Customs House designed by Waterford man James Ryan is built on the Quay.

1876 CE: The Theatre Royal opens for the first time with Mr John Royston's Comedy and Opera Bouffe Company. It is taken over by Waterford Corporation in 1881.

1877 CE: On 6 February, Isaac Butt is the first person to be bestowed the freedom of the city since the Waterford Corporation was reformed in 1842.

1880 CE: Charles Stewart Parnell speaks at a demonstration held at Ballybricken on 5 December. The following day he is awarded the freedom of the city.

1884 CE: The Holy Ghost Hospital opens on the Cork Road. In the same year, the Pig Buyers' Association is founded.

1892 CE: The construction of the Good Shepherd Convent at College Street commences and is completed in 1894.

1894 CE: De La Salle College is opened.

1895 CE: A Waterford horse, *The Wild Man from Borneo,* owned by John Widger, trained by Michael Widger and ridden by his brother Joe, wins the Grand National at Aintree on 29 March.

1900 CE: Last execution in Ballybricken Jail on 10 April. On 10 August, the first Sisters of Mercy school in Waterford opens at Philip Street.

1904 CE: On 2 May, King Edward VII visits Waterford.

1906 CE: The Central Technical Institute opens on 1 October at Parnell Street.

1908 CE: In October, the labour leader James Larkin speaks at City Hall.

1909 CE: The Waterford Trades Council meets for the first time on 24 May.

1912 CE: Dr Mary Strangman is the first woman elected to the Waterford Corporation, on 15 January. She is followed shortly after by Mrs Lily Poole on 22 February. In the same year, Redmond Bridge (costing £64,000) is opened to pedestrians on New Year's Eve. It is officially opened by John Redmond MP, on 10 February 1913.

Waterford, as a commercial place, has an appearance of opulence, superior to any of the sea-ports we have visited.

J.C. Curwen, 1813

Although Waterford is a mercantile city and one with advantages peculiarly eligible and accessible, there is a sad aspect of loneliness in its streets and a want of business along its quays, except on those days when the steam-boats embark for the English market. The hotels, too, usually sure indications of prosperity or its opposite, have a deserted look and it would hardly an exaggeration to say that the grass springs up between the steps that lead to their doors.

Mr and Mrs Charles Hall (Travel writers, 1840s)

Presently we caught sight of the valley through which the Suir flows, and descended the hill towards it, and went over the thundering old wooden bridge to Waterford. The view of the town from the bridge and the heights above is very imposing, as is the river both ways. Very large vessels sail up almost to the doors of the houses, and the quays are flanked by tall red warehouses, that look at a little distance as if a world of business might be doing within them, But as you get into the place, not a soul is there to greet you, except the usual society of beggars, and a sailor or two, or a green-coated policeman sauntering down the broad pavement.

William Makepeace Thackeray, *An Irish Sketchbook*, 1842

[The city's people were] ... easy-going, light-hearted, frank, generous, but too much given to trivial amusements, and too apt to let things drift. They do not seem to think for themselves, and like to follow the example of their neighbour whether it be right or wrong.

United Irishman, 1905

MEMBERS OF PARLIAMENT FOR WATERFORD CITY

Election	1st Member	Party	2nd Member	Party
1801	William Congreve Alcock	Tory		
24 July 1803	Sir Simon John Newport	Whig		
Representation increased to two members 1832				
21 December 1832	Henry Winston Barron	Repeal Association	William Christmas	Conservative
17 January 1835			Thomas Wyse	Liberal
12 July 1841★	William Christmas	Conservative	William Morris Reade	Conservative
13 June 1842	Sir Henry Winston Barron	Liberal	Thomas Wyse	Liberal
4 August 1847	Thomas Meagher	Repeal Association	Daniel O'Connell Jr.	Repeal Association
1 March 1848 By-Election			Sir Henry Winston Barron	Liberal
15 July 1852			Robert Keating	Liberal
2 April 1857	John Aloysius Blake	Ind. Irish	Michael Dobbyn Hassard	Conservative
13 July 1865		Liberal	Sir Henry Winston Barron	Liberal
20 November 1868			James Delahunty	Liberal
22 November 1869 By-Election	Sir Henry Winston Barron	Liberal		
25 February 1870 By-Election	Ralph Bernal Osborne	Liberal		

6 February 1874	Richard Power	Home Rule League	Purcell O'Gorman	Home Rule League
April 1880			Edmund Leamy	Home Rule League
1882		Irish Parliamentary Party		Irish Parliamentary Party
Representation Reduced to One Member 1885				
1885	Richard Power	Nationalist		
1890		Parnellite		
17 December 1891 *By-election*	John Edward Redmond	Irish Parliamentary Party		
22 March 1918 *By-Election*	William Archer Redmond	Irish Parliamentary Party		

WATERFORD AND NEWFOUNDLAND

Waterford's trading connections with Newfoundland continued and from 1809 to 1815 there was increased movement of people and commodities (primarily cod), though the conclusion of the Napoleonic Wars led to a decline in the economy and trade. Newfoundland was known to the Irish as *Talamh an Éisec* ('land of fish') which drew fishermen from the south-east of Ireland from the middle of the seventeenth century. From 1800 to 1830 around 30,000 to 35,000 people migrated to Newfoundland, many from Waterford, which has led to the development of what is called 'Newfie' culture and a peculiarly accented English with a strong Irish influence.

EDMUND RICE AND THE CHRISTIAN BROTHERS

Frank Heylin states that the 'period of Waterford's greatness in mercantile affairs happened to coincide with the merchant life of Edmund Rice in the

City'. Due to the poor living conditions of the urban poor, Rice sought to help the young men and boys through education. The period saw Waterford establish connections with Newfoundland through shipping. Up to 5,000 people would travel there every year. Ballybricken was a centre of activity, with fairs being held. Alcohol was indulged following the tradition where under Municipal Law the city's inhabitants could distil whiskey for their own consumption.

Edmund Rice established the Christian Brothers and founded his first school in Waterford, named Mount Sion, in 1802. This was the beginning of an educational movement that spread across Ireland and the world.

Rice was born in Callan, County Kilkenny, on 1 June 1762. He moved to Waterford City to work for his uncle who exported goods, later inheriting the business. Marrying in 1785, the turning point in Rice's life was the death of his wife in 1789 from a riding accident, which led to the premature birth of his disabled daughter.

Edmund Ignatius Rice was founder of the Congregation of Christian Brothers and the Presentation Brothers.

The Callan native left business and contemplated joining an enclosed order. Rice saw his vocation in helping the destitute of Waterford City. He established a school for poor boys and later developed a school and monastery in the city around 1802. Rice founded the order named the Institute of the Brothers of Christian Schools, known as the Christian Brothers, which was approved by Pope Pius VII in 1820. By the time Rice retired in 1838, the Christian Brothers consisted of twenty-two houses in Ireland and England. He died in Mount Sion on 29 August 1844.

WATERFORD:
The Kennedy Connection

The lineage of American presidents can be traced through bloodlines, and one of the most well known is that of John Fitzgerald Kennedy and his family's connection to New Ross in County Wexford. Yet less well known are the tragic and still slightly mysterious circumstances by which his ancestor reached the New World. The tale of Kennedy's Waterford connection begins with a Mr William Congreve Alcock.

Alcock was a Member of Parliament for Waterford City from 1797 to 1800. He opposed the Act of Union and was considered the leading figure in the city proposing resistance to it. Alcock was re-elected in 1801 and 1802 but was unseated upon petition the following year. He eventually stood for the parliament seat at Wexford in 1807 against Abel Ram, John Colclough and Richard Brinsley Sheridan. Colclough (brother of Caesar Colclough of Tintern Abbey) and Alcock argued over the poaching of votes, which resulted in a duel on 30 May 1807. Watched by the county sheriff and sixteen magistrates, Colclough was killed in the first exchange of fire. Alcock was acquitted of murder but the incident triggered a terrible depression as his mental health declined.(He was consigned to Thomas Warburton lunatic asylum.) This became apparent to the government, when he commanded the patronage of Waterford City (while being an MP for Wexford). He died on 4 September 1813.

The duel not only precipitated the decline of Alcock but left the estate of Tintern Abbey in the care of the steward James Kennedy (from whom JFK descends) in the absence of Caesar Colclough. The deceased's brother returned to Ireland from France in 1815 when it was noted that £80,000 had disappeared. The money was never accounted for nor was anyone held to task. Kennedy was dismissed as the steward of Tintern in 1818. Historian and broadcaster Myles Dungan writes:

> There are, however, persistent rumours that at least some of it may have been used a generation later to fund the migration to the USA of the Kennedy family in the 1840s, and perhaps even to set up the Boston saloon that became the basis of the family fortune.

JFK became President of the United States of America in 1961. And it seems that his family's wealth may have been started on the basis of a duel involving a Waterford man.

CHARLES KEAN:
Shakespearean Actor

Charles John Kean was born in Colbeck Street (in the same house as William Vincent Wallace, the composer), Waterford City on 18 January 1811. He was the second son of Edmund Kean, the renowned Shakespearean actor, and Mary Chambers, an actress from Waterford. His father and mother divorced around 1825, forcing Charles to leave Eton at the age of 16. He decided to become an actor, after his father's failure to pay a £400 settlement to his mother, which led Charles to turn down the offer of a cadetship by the East India Company in 1827. Charles first appeared on stage at Drury Lane, but left London by the spring of 1828 for the provinces to achieve the fame and acclaim he hungered for. Success would follow with his performance in *Romeo and Juliet* in 1829 at London Haymarket, followed by a successful tour of *Richard III* in the United States. However, his zenith would be his role as *Hamlet* in 1838 at Drury Lane, which made him one of the great tragic actors of the age.

Kean returned to his hometown in 1836 and was presented with a claret jug (valued at more than £100) by a group of amateur actors. On learning of the destruction of the New Theatre Royal at Bolton Street by accidental fire in April 1837, Kean wrote a letter to the manager of the theatre, a Mr F. Seymour:

Charles Kean as Hamlet in 1838. Son of renowned actor Edmund Kean, Charles was best remembered for his revivals of Shakespearean plays.

I deeply deplore the calamity that has befallen you, and trust sincerely my townspeople will not be behind hand in giving you every assistance in their power to extricate you from the difficulties such a loss must have occasioned you. For my part I am willing to play in a barn, if you will fit it up, and may depend on my commencing tour with you early in June, but the precise date I cannot at present name, but in a fortnight I will arrange everything with you definitely. Cork, I think, would be the best town for the opening. In Waterford I shall be most happy to afford you my gratuitous services for a benefit, and in the hope that you will be enabled to fit up the Town Hall, and that circumstances will not turn out so badly as you anticipate.

Charles Kean married Ellen Tree in 1842. There were tours in the United States between 1845 and 1847. In 1851, he became the manager of the Princess Theatre, which staged a series of successful Shakespearean revivals. Kean retired from acting in 1859 for the first time, and instigated a tour of the US, Jamaica and Australia with his wife in 1863, returning to England by 1866. Kean's final treading of 'the boards' was in Liverpool in 1867. He died in Chelsea on 2 January 1868.

WILLIAM VINCENT WALLACE:
Opera Composer

Born in Waterford on 11 March 1812 at Colbeck Street, Wallace showcased his talent as an organist in the city. His skills as a violinist were demonstrated in Dublin as a teenager. He married Isabella Kelly in 1831. Three years later he performed a concerto of his own composing in Dublin. A year later he travelled to Australia (for health reasons) and became the first significant musician to perform in the country.

By 1840–41, Wallace settled in North America and had been parted from his wife since his journey to Australia. Wallace was a member of the

Bust of opera composer William Vincent Wallace adjacent to the Theatre Royal.

Philharmonic Society in New York and later became a conductor of an Italian opera season in Mexico. The midpoint of the decade saw him tour Germany and Holland before reaching London in March 1845, where his opera *Maritana* was staged at Drury Lane.

The 1850s saw Wallace's operas in great demand in London. The year 1860 saw his opera *Lurline* performed at Covent Garden and deemed a major success. The failing of his health led Wallace to the Pyrenees where he died on 12 October 1865. His remains are interred at Kensal Green Cemetery in London. In total, Wallace composed ten operas, with the six published being *Maritana* (1845), *Matilda of Hungary* (1847), *Lurline* (1860), *The Amber Witch* (1861), *Love's Triumph* (1862) and *Desert Flower* (1863).

SIR (SIMON) JOHN NEWPORT AND THE CORPORATION COMPACT, 10 JUNE 1818

Sir (Simon) John Newport was born in Waterford in 1756 (coincidentally the same year his father John became mayor of the city). He would go on to be educated at Eton, and would enter the Irish bar after a time at Lincoln's Inn (though he did not ever practice), and by 1789 was made a baronet. He came to prominence in his native city when he became an alderman of the corporation and was a part of the committee that was empowered to deal with the construction of a bridge over the River Suir in the 1780s and early 1790s.

At heart, Newport was a liberal who supported Catholic relief in 1792, and believed that Catholic Emancipation would be achieved through the Act of Union which he favoured. By 1803, Newport would become an MP for Waterford City, which he represented until 1832, the same year as the Parliamentary Reform Act. Newport made an electoral pact with the Alcock family in June 1818 guaranteeing him a safe seat until his retirement in 1832.

In the House of Commons, he aligned himself with William Wyndham Grenville's Whig regime. His family business of banking would lead him to become the primary spokesperson on Irish finances, and a fervent critic of Irish budgets while in opposition. Another issue he devoted his political career to was the abolition of the slave trade. However, his activities in Westminster would be curtailed upon the collapse of the Newport family bank. It appears that Newport's creditors were not compensated, though he was regulator of the exchequer in the intervening years, 1832 to 1839, receiving a wage of £1,000 annually. In 1830, he declined a position in government when the Grenvillites aligned themselves with Lord Liverpool, due to the reluctance of the Liverpool administration to have dealt previously with the issue of Catholic Emancipation. On 9 February 1843, Newport died in Waterford.

HENRY DENNY AND THE BACON RASHER

The bacon rasher was invented by Waterford butcher Henry Denny in 1820. Until Denny's innovation, pork had been placed in barrels full of brine to be cured. To increase the longevity of the meat, Henry Denny sandwiched long flat pieces of pork between layers of dry salt. Not only did Denny's technique of curing pork change the meat industry in Ireland, but his idea received much acclaim and admiration in other countries. Henry Denny's name lives on in the company that bears his name. 'Denny's' would go on to invent the skinless sausage in 1941.

WATERFORD STEAMSHIP COMPANY

In 1826, the Waterford and Bristol Steam Navigation Company was established. The Waterford Steamship Company's head office was located on the Mall in the city centre. Available routes included local services to Youghal in County Cork via Dungarvan, New Ross and Duncannon in County Wexford. The most popular (and financially successful) sailings were to Bristol and Liverpool across the Irish Sea. Such demand led to not only increased services but a rise in the cost of fares. By 1877 for the Waterford–Liverpool run, the price of a cabin was 17s 6d, while a deck fare was 10s for adults and 5s for children. A journey to London was also an available route with the Waterford Steamship Company via Plymouth. They were able to offer the facility of carrying goods for Portsmouth and Southampton. However, by the end of the decade this service had been dispensed with. Other weekly services included Newport (inaugurated in 1879) in Wales and Belfast. Some of the steamships owned by the company carried names with local relevance such as *Reginald* and *Comeragh*. By the end of the 1870s, the only routes to survive were its local services and routes to Bristol and Liverpool. The company had acquired the wooden paddle steamer the *Water Witch* which was built at Birkenhead in 1883. The steamer was considered 'the fastest vessel that ever floated' at the time.

THE PENITENTIARY

The Penitentiary, designed by James Elmes, was constructed by the builder Thomas Anthony at Hennessy's Road in 1820, costing £4,990. It replaced the House of Correction which was kept by Thomas Adamson, who in 1702 was permitted £2 per annum and sixpence for every prisoner flogged by him at the mayor's request. A depiction of the new Penitentiary from Samuel Lewis in 1839 details:

> An exterior wall surrounds a quadrangular space of considerable extent, at one extremity of which is the Governor's house, having the cells ranged in a semicircle round it. At the rear of the cells, and within the walls, are gardens and grounds, where the prisoners are regularly employed. There are in all 41 cells and airing yards, in one of which is a treadmill adapted to four distinct classes. The whole prison is under a regular system of discipline and employment, and a school is maintained for the instruction of the prisoners.

From June 1821 to April 1824, the Penitentiary received 269 prisoners with the average cost of the establishment coming to £260.

WATERFORD AND CATHOLIC EMANCIPATION

Thomas Meagher, originally of Newfoundland, resided with his wife Alicia in a Georgian house on the quay (where the Granville Hotel now stands) which was subsequently leased to the Italian carriage entrepreneur Charles Bianconi, who adapted it as a stagecoach station. The Meaghers moved eventually to Derrynane House on the Mall, named after the birthplace of Daniel O'Connell. Waterford was sympathetic to the cause of O'Connell, and Catholic Emancipation was eventually achieved when the Kerryman entered the Westminster Parliament in 1830, the first Catholic to achieve this feat.

The momentum from this led to a campaign for Repeal of the Union. Meagher, an ardent supporter of O'Connell, became the first Catholic Mayor of Waterford in well over a century. The movement received financial support from the Irish Diaspora in Newfoundland. The second Catholic to be elected to the parliament in London was Waterford-born Thomas Wyse (in 1830 representing Tipperary). Wyse broke away from the Repeal of the Union movement and became influential in educational reform with the creation of the national school system.

'A MOST APPALLING MISERY':
Waterford, Disease and Famine in the Nineteenth Century

Migration continued between Waterford and Newfoundland, allowing for individuals to improve their social status while providing opportunity for those to work outside the city. This connection proved to be life-saving: it is one of the reasons why the Great Hunger was not as damaging in Waterford City compared to the rest of the island. There was still poverty in the city prior to the Famine, with Englishman Henry D. Inglis writing in 1834: 'I visited some of the worst quarters of the town, and was introduced to scenes of most appalling misery.' As the wealthier classes left the city centre to live in mansions outside Waterford's confines, the Georgian houses they emptied became slums, leading to overcrowding which was worsened when people from rural areas sought relief in the city. Such poor conditions contributed to an outbreak of cholera in 1832.

To combat cholera, the local corporation sought to build new sewers, widen streets and improve the city's water supply. The latter half of the century saw the corporation's first housing scheme at Green Street where seventeen two-storey houses were constructed between 1878 and 1879.

The blight of the potato crop in the 1840s impacted rural Ireland greatly as it was a staple part of their diet. To provide relief for the struggling population, a workhouse was established in Waterford City at John's Hill where the poor could be catered for. *An Introduction to the Architectural Heritage of County Waterford* states: 'Waterford City hosted the greatest variety and number of substantial public buildings, including those built for the welfare of others [in County Waterford in the nineteenth century].' By March 1847 there were 1,063 people in the Waterford Workhouse. In the summer of the same year, the number of fever cases was at its worst, leading to a temporary fever hospital being established in the city. A major impact of *An Gorta Mor* (the Great Hunger) was the decline in population due to deaths and emigration. With Waterford being a substantial urban area, it led to many coming from more destitute rural areas in search of relief. In 1841, the population of the city stood at 23,216, rising to 25,297 by 1851. While the 1850s saw continued migration, the population for the entire county of Waterford declined.

THOMAS FRANCIS MEAGHER:
Irish Patriot and American Civil War Combatant

Born on 3 August 1823 in Waterford City, Meagher was educated at Clongowes Wood College in Kildare and at Stonyhurst in England. In 1843, he returned to Waterford and followed his father's lead (an O'Connellite MP and Mayor of Waterford 1842–44) by supporting Daniel O'Connell's Repeal of the Union movement. After deserting his legal studies, he became heavily involved in the Repeal Association. In 1846, as part of the Young Ireland movement, they broke away from O'Connell's group, the former arguing for the use of physical force. As an Irish Confederation candidate, he ran in the Waterford City by-election of February 1848. (The theme of fathers and sons comes to mind; Meagher competed for the vacant seat in his father's constituency which occurred when the son of Daniel O'Connell took up a position in government.) He did not win the seat.

He was nicknamed 'Meagher of the Sword', which was concocted by William Makepeace Thackeray in *Punch* after the Waterford man gave a speech to repeal the Act of Union on 28 July 1846. The following quote comes from *The Nation* (1 August 1846):

Abhor the sword and stigmatize the sword? No, my lord, for in the cragged passes of the Tyrol it cut in pieces the banner of the Bavarian, and won the immortality for the peasant of Innsbruck.

Abhor the sword and stigmatize the sword? No, my lord, for at a blow a giant nation sprung up from the waters of the far Atlantic, and by its redeeming magic the fettered colony became a daring free republic.

A supporter of the new French Revolution, Meagher travelled to France in 1848 (while on bail), returning with what would become the Irish tricolour. He returned to Ireland to mount a rising which ended in failure. He was eventually arrested at Cashel in August and charged with high treason. Initially sentenced to death, this was commuted to transportation, leaving Ireland in 1849 for Tasmania. While there, he married Catherine Bennett in 1851. The following year he travelled to New York and was warmly welcomed by the Irish-American community.

In the subsequent years, he was admitted to the New York bar, worked as a newspaper publisher and as an orator. His wife Catherine had died in Waterford in 1854 (as a result of giving birth to their second son; their first had died four months after being born in 1852). In 1856, he married Elizabeth Townsend and lived in her family home. By the end of the 1850s, James Stephens sought Meagher's support for his newly established Irish Republican Brotherhood and Fenian movement, but was to leave disappointed. On the outbreak of the American Civil War, Meagher, a supporter of the union, was commissioned captain of the

Thomas Francis Meagher, Irish nationalist and leader of the Young Irelanders during the rebellion of 1848. He flew the Irish tricolour for the first time at the Wolfe Tone Club in Waterford on 7 March 1848.

William Makepeace Thackeray (steel engraving by Smith, Elder & Co., 1853).

Statue of Thomas Francis Meagher located on the Mall in Waterford city centre.

69th Regiment. However, his military capabilities were rather questionable and would leave a mark on his legacy. Having alienated a lot of Irish-American supporters by his actions and backing Abraham Lincoln in the 1864 presidential election, he sought a government position from the subsequent Johnson presidency.

As acting governor of Montana (then not a state), his time there was as controversial as it was brief. In trying to establish law and order, he died in mysterious circumstances. On 1 July 1867, as part of containing hostilities with the Sioux Indians, he fell overboard from a steamer on the Missouri River, the details of which are a matter of conjecture and gossip. E.P. Cunningham concludes that in 'each of his multiple careers … he made a mark'.

Meagher wrote of his native city:

Waterford never appeared to me to change. For a century at least, it has not gained a wrinkle nor lost a smile. In every season, and for a thousand seasons, it has been and will be the same old tree. If no fresh leaf springs, no dead leaf drops from it. The Danes planted it; Strongbow put his name and that of Eva, his Irish bride, deep into its bark; and King John held court beneath its boughs; James the Second hid his crown into the crevices of its roots, and fled from it to France. It has witnessed many other events; many other familiarities have been taken with it. Many worse blows have been given it, since the Earl of Pembroke hacked it with his sword. But it has suffered nothing. The dews, and the storms, and the frost, and the summer heat, have come and pass away, hurting nothing; improving nothing; leaving it, at the end of ages, the same old dusty, quiet, hearty, bounteous, venerable tree. Heaven bless it! And may the sweet birds long fill its shady trellises with music; and the noble stream with full breast nourish the earth where it has root!

THE TEMPERANCE MOVEMENT IN WATERFORD, 1839–41

Waterford, prior to the Temperance Movement, was one of the places where alcohol was often abused. In 1838, it was believed that thirteen pints of spirits were drunk per person in Ireland. In total, Waterford City had three distilleries at the start of the century (but all would close due to new government regulations). The impact of this can be seen in the records of Waterford General Dispensary, with admittance figures at 5,708 in 1811; this high number of patients was due in part to low drink prices.

By the 1830s, there were 190 public houses in Waterford. Near the end of the decade it was estimated that nearly 6,000 gallons of whiskey were consumed in Waterford every year. Poteen would also have been widely available in the city at half the price of legal whiskey. In the last three months of 1838, 964 people were arrested in Waterford City for being drunk.

The efforts to tackle the problem in Waterford began in May 1830, when a meeting at the Town Hall sought to found the Waterford Temperance Society. However, it wasn't a great success – one attendee argued that total abstinence discriminated against moderate drinkers. Shockingly, the proposal that members of the group could consume alcohol on a moderate basis was passed and the group was never formally formed.

A juvenile temperance group was established by Brother Patrick Joseph Murphy of Mount Sion in 1835, predating the movement popularised by Father Theobald Matthew by three years. On 10 November 1839, the Waterford branch of Fr Matthew's Total Abstinence Association was formed at Mount Sion school. Regular meetings would be held there, and there was a resolution to open a coffee shop. There was no repeat of the shambolic first attempt to establish such a movement in the city, though alcohol was permitted purely for medicinal purposes.

Fr Matthew visited the city on 11 December 1839, with some estimating that a crowd of between 30,000 to 40,000 were present to take the pledge. The gathering would descend into violence when the crowd attacked the police who were escorting Matthew to the courthouse for his own safety. He continued to administer the pledge there, where only 200 people were permitted in the building at any one time. Over his two-day visit to the city it is believed up to 70,000 people took the pledge with some having travelled from counties such as Kildare and Wicklow. During the visit, it was the first time in twenty years that no member of the public had been imprisoned in Reginald's Tower for drunkenness. That Christmas, a procession of 12,000 people marched from Ballybricken to the bishop's house in the name of the Temperance Society. The 1840s began with another procession which was 7,000 strong. The St Patrick's Day parade that year saw 20,000 people march under the Temperance movement banner in front of around 3,000 spectators.

The Apostle of Temperance returned again in May 1840, with up to 24,000 people undertaking the pledge. The Waterford Teetotal Temperance Society had grown from 50 to 15,000 members. The Waterford Protestant Temperance Society could boast 500 members. This group operated on the basis of temperance movements pre-Matthew and felt alienated by the increasing Catholic tone and symbols used by such groups. Fr Walter O'Brien noted in the Catholic Bulletin in 1924 that of Matthew: 'he accomplished as great a work for Ireland as did Daniel O'Connell, but because his work was moral, not political, he is almost forgotten'.

'LIKE A PEARL IN ITS MOUTH':
Johann Georg Kohl's Observations on Waterford

The Bremen-born Johann Georg Kohl toured Ireland in 1842, with his musings translated and published in English the following year. He arrived in Ireland on 22 September at Holyhead, which started his month-long travels around the country. Kohl describes his first view of Waterford as follows:

> We soon after beheld the valley of the Suir, the lofty picturesque shore of rock on both its sides, and the beautifully situated town of Waterford, like a pearl in its mouth.

Johann Georg Kohl was a Bremen-born German travel writer who wrote about visiting Waterford City.

He notes how the population of the city had virtually been static. It was the sixth largest city on the island, of around 30,000 people by the start of the 1840s, and in 1821 having a population of 28,676 and increased by 145 ten years later. Kohl suggests that the 8 per cent population increase proved that 'the principal increase of population does not take place in the towns, but in the country' in Ireland. Yet exports had more than doubled in the city, grain being acknowledged as the main product.

In addition, Kohl suggests that core to the growth in exports was:

> First, one of the most wonderful quays in the world; and secondly, one of the finest harbours in Ireland. The quay is a mile long, and so broad and convenient withal, that it must be invaluable to merchants and mariners. It is skirted by a row of elegant houses; and the scenery on the opposite of the river, which is here a mile and a half wide, is extremely picturesque. The embouchure of the river Suir, which forms the harbour, is wide and deep, without islands or sandbanks, and affords all possible security convenience to ships.

While dining in a 'Repeal Room' of a hotel, he details the three newspapers published in Waterford that supported O'Connell's movement. He manages to sketch a brief history of Waterford from Strongbow to Oliver Cromwell. From Waterford, Kohl proceeds to New Ross on his journey of Ireland.

MONSTER MEETING AT BALLYBRICKEN, JULY 1843

Early July 1843 would see people from all over the south-east of Ireland descend on Ballybricken to hear from Daniel O'Connell. Chaired by Sir Richard Musgrave, members of the Temperance Society dressed in 'blue cloth, turned up with white and crimson' were in attendance. A stage for O'Connell was erected on the hill of Ballybricken. To the estimated crowd of 300,000 O'Connell proceeded to attack Villiers-Stuart for not aligning to the campaign of Repeal of the Union. He admonished the County Waterford MP further by declaring him a 'featherbrained representative'. Also highlighted was the situation in which the franchise could be obtained in the city for £10 compared with 1/- in Bristol. He believed that in reaching parity with conditions in England, Villiers-Stuart had failed to 'explain to us what prospect we had of achieving such a consummation in the English house of Legislature'.

When the speech concluded, a dinner was held in City Hall for 450 (paying) supporters. The celebrations were led by Mayor Thomas Meagher with toasts made to O'Connell and the Royal Family. O'Connell noted that 'this was the most glorious day of his existence' and festivities came to a finish at one o'clock in the morning.

THE MALCOLMSONS:
an Entrepreneurial Family

Bill Irish states, 'Waterford retained a pre-eminence in ship-building by becoming a leading centre of iron ship-building, due mainly to the vision, initiative, enterprise and courage of the Malcolmsons.' Of Scottish descent, the Malcolmsons' enterprising empire began when brothers John (born in 1761) and David (born in 1765) established a corn mill on Suir Island, Clonmel (costing £3,000). The latter brother married Mary Fennel of Cahir Abbey in 1795. Under David, it would expand to include mills and stores at Carrick-on-Suir. In trying to establish a cotton mill in Portlaw in 1825, David Malcolmson spent £60,000 on the construction of a canal joining the rivers Clodagh and Suir to create access to the mill by barge. In 1844, David died, leaving his business to his eldest son, Joseph. The Malcolmson brothers' interests in railways, coal (they owned their own mine in the Ruhr Valley, Germany) and shipping led to them entering the shipbuilding business with Neptune Shipping. The Neptune shipyard and the fall of the Malcolmson business empire will be looked at later in this chapter.

THE FAMINE IN WATERFORD, 1845–52

Bishop Robert Daly was involved in famine relief in the city by going door to door with tickets for food, clothing and coal. Professor Desmond Bowen states that Daly 'laboured heroically on behalf of the starving people' during the period. Similarly, the Quakers in Waterford formed a Relief Committee made up of prominent business families in the city, such as the Strangmans. Quaker women had visited 900 of the city's inhabitants and by January 1847 provided a litre of soup with bread to 580 poverty-stricken people four times a week.

Inevitably, the price of the potato increased in Waterford, reaching the amount of 21*d* for a stone of the vegetable in September 1847. Also, the price of flour increased by 30 per cent by 1846 from pre-famine cost. John M. Hearne notes in a special edition of the *Decies* journal in 1995 devoted to the famine that 'while wage levels may have been adequate in pre-famine years, by late 1846 and 1847 escalating food prices, especially of those items that were significant in the staple diet, potatoes and offal, made them look insignificant'. A letter from the Waterford Chamber of Commerce to British Prime Minister Peel outlined that the 'labouring population of this city … are now for the most part in a state of deplorable destitution … while the heavy pressure on the poor is aggravated by the general deficiency of employment'.

A government measure of public works sought to rectify these conditions. Devised by Charles Trevelyan, the new scheme saw local corporations bear the cost of the works (compared to the British government covering half the costs as prior to 1846), the logic being that 'Irish poverty was to be supported by Irish property'. These schemes would be carried out by the Board of Works. In the case of Waterford City, the Waterford Relief Committee held a meeting at City Hall on 28 September 1846 to explore possible public works which would improve the city. It was resolved that there should be an improvement in the water supply to the city; that a number of lanes off Barronstrand Street be enlarged; and the appointment of a person to investigate the necessity of a public cemetery. Subsequently, a session at the Court House saw the presentation of the levelling of the marketplace at Ballybricken; changing the course of the Pill; and numerous road, pump and sewer proposals across the city. However, there were not enough funds to permit all the desired developments. Dermot Power writes:

> The public relief works had cost £4,848, £235 2*s* 6*d* – all of which was to be paid out of local rates. It was decided to reduce the numbers employed on public works by 20 percent on March 20, and the schemes were to be shut down completely by May 1. It would appear that the rate payers and magistrates of Waterford City were deeply touched by the hunger and want

around them, and indeed were caring people with a genuine desire to alleviate the great hunger and distress caused by the Famine in Waterford City.

The knock-on effect of such destitution was emigration. By 1847, forty-three ships had sailed to North America from Waterford. The following year would see thirty-four ships accomplishing the same journey, with nearly 1,000 people leaving per week by 1849.

FREDERICK DOUGLASS AND WATERFORD CITY, 9 OCTOBER 1845

I can truly say, I have spent some of the happiest moments of my life since landing in this country, I seem to have undergone a transformation. I live a new life.

Frederick Douglass

In August 1845, Frederick Douglass left Boston for a lecture tour of Britain and Ireland. Douglass had escaped slavery in Maryland in 1837, reaching Massachusetts, and became a skilled orator and proponent of the abolition of slavery. He was sponsored by the American Anti-Slavery Society to travel and speak of his experiences. Douglass' first book, *Narrative of the Life of Frederick Douglass, an American slave* was published in the spring of 1845. The tour to Europe was partly to publicise the book as well as allowing for tensions surrounding its publication to calm in the United States.

First reaching Liverpool, Douglass took a ferry to Dublin, in a trip that he intended 'to increase my stock of information, and my opportunities for self-improvement, by a visit to the land of my paternal ancestors'. He believed that his father was a 'white man'.

While in Ireland, Douglass travelled to Dublin, Cork, Limerick and Belfast, with stops at Waterford and Wexford. He spoke with notable figures such as the 'Liberator' Daniel O'Connell and Father Matthew of the Temperance Movement. He travelled as the impact of the failure of the potato crop was starting to devastate the island. He spoke at the Large Room in City Hall on 9 October 1845.

On his return to the United States, Douglass represented the trip to Ireland as broadening his political thoughts and saw parallels with the predicament with the Irish people and that of the African American. This can be seen in his article in *Atlantic Monthly* in 1867 when he noted 'what O'Connell said of the history of Ireland may with greater truth be said of the negro's. It may be traced like a wounded man through a crowd, by the blood.' He went on to provide counsel to President Abraham Lincoln during the American Civil War and campaigned for the preservation of the union and an end to slavery.

Douglass died in Washington DC on 20 February 1895.

Frederick Douglass, c. 1866. Douglass said that 'the cause of humanity is one the world over'. *Collection of New York Historical Society.*

NO. 33 THE MALL

Originally a townhouse for the Carew family constructed in the late Georgian era, this building became the headquarters of the local Irish nationalist independence movement and was named the Wolfe Tone Confederate Club. The four-storey bow-fronted building was the location for meetings of the Young Irelander movement in the city. It is believed to be the site where the Irish tricolour of green, white and orange was first flown on 7 March 1848 by Thomas Francis Meagher. He was presented with the flag made from French silk, and stated:

> I trust that the old country will not refuse this symbol of a new life from one of her youngest children. I need not explain its meaning. The quick and passionate intellect of the generation now springing into arms will catch it at a glance. The white in the centre signifies a lasting truce between the 'orange' and the 'green' and I trust beneath its folds, the hands of the Irish Protestant and the Irish Catholic may be clasped in generous and heroic brotherhood …

In the 1970s, the building was significantly renovated, and in more recent times has been a tobacconist, a nightclub and a café.

REVITALISATION OF SHIPBUILDING IN WATERFORD CITY

The development of steamships in the nineteenth century lead to a revival of shipbuilding in Waterford. The first such vessel to be recorded on the River Suir was in June 1817: the *Princess Charlotte,* built by the Clyde Shipping Company in 1814. By the end of the century a ratio of five out of six ships across the globe were built in either Britain or Ireland. Such scale and high level of demand impacted the Quaysides in Waterford. On the Ferrybank side of the river, there were shipyards operated by Whites and Pope and Co. in the 1820s. In total, four shipyards were in existence at Ferrybank until 1865 (at one stage three at the same time) constructing sixty vessels. One such yard was Penrose, situated at the pier head adjacent to the flour mills.

Also in the 1850s was the Charles Smith Shipyard which specialised in smaller 200- to 300-ton ships. Such was the scope of the yard that the ship *Pathfinder,* launched 1 May 1858, was used in the copper ore trade on the west coast of South America. In addition, they constructed wooden lifeboats for steamers made by Neptune Shipping in the early years of that company.

White's yard was located between Timbertoes bridge and McCullagh's wharf. Two of the more notable ships to come from this yard were the *Madge Wilere* and the *Merrie England* which were owned by the founder of the British Shipowners Company, James Beasley, an inhabitant of Liverpool.

Pope and County Shipyard originally manufactured vessels to facilitate the Pope family's trading with Britain and later for small shipowners. Undoubtedly, the most renowned ship from this yard was the SS *Kilkenny*. Built in 1837, it was purchased by the East India Company two years later and renamed *Zenobia*. Waterford maritime historian Bill Irish noted of this steamer that it 'was one of the first steamships to make the passage around the Cape of Good Hope to India'.

In 1841, Waterford and Cork accounted for 41 per cent of the ships built in Ireland. The Neptune Ironworks was opened in 1843 by Joseph Malcolmson Bros as a repair yard for their steamships. In 1847, they launched their own vessel, the SS *Neptune,* the first of forty ships built at the yard until 1882. This steamer became the first such vessel to regularly service the London–St Petersburg route. On her journey up the Neva, she was boarded by Tsar Nicholas I who ordered that whenever this ship was stationed at Petersburg it did not have to pay its port tariffs.

With the Malcolmsons' interests in the Cork and Waterford Steamship companies (which they controlled) and the P&O Line (as a shareholder), the yard under the stewardship of Joseph Malcolmson went from strength to strength. A visionary, in 1847 Joseph had previously purchased the screw steamer *Dublin,* the first such vessel to be owned by an Irish company. Obviously, this experience aided them in convincing P&O to switch to screw propulsion. In 1858, the SS *Cuba* became the first ever four 'masted' steamship in the world, continuing a tradition of progression and innovation by the yard.

By the 1860s, the Neptune yard employed up to 400 workers, with new vessels constructed every nine months. They constructed the largest ship ever built in Ireland until that point in 1882. The *Cella* was 300ft long and cost £33,500 to manufacture. It was subsequently sold to owners based in Constantinople and renamed *Sharki*. An ordinary labourer earned ten shillings a week on construction of the vessel, while a carpenter earned nearly three times as much. The day of its launch saw huge crowds in attendance as the ferry brought 1,600 people, and a seventeen-carriage train from Limerick came for the festivities. The 1870s saw the yard specialise in steam yachts.

However, outside factors would come to play a part in the demise of Neptune. A naval blockade of ports in the south of the United States led to a decline in raw cotton resources. This combined with the building of several Malcolmson family houses in Dunmore East, Portlaw and Clonmel, and the family's bankers, Overund and Gurney of London, which had run up debts up to £13 million, went bankrupt. In 1877, Malcolmson Bros too declared themselves bankrupt. Yet Neptune fulfilled orders, completing its last ship in 1882, a steam yacht named *Maritana*.

THE RAILWAYS OF WATERFORD CITY

The late Waterford historian Jack O'Neill described the railway as 'the major instrument in transforming the economy and society in nineteenth-century Ireland'. Over 2,000 people in Waterford were in employment with railway services by the start of the twentieth century. In total, five railways operated to and from Waterford City by 1900. In 1826 (the year in which the first ever railway line between Stockton and Darlington was built), a railway line between Waterford and Limerick was mooted, for building to commence over twenty years later. The first section of the line from Limerick to Tipperary was completed in 1848 and reached Fiddown, County Kilkenny, by 1852. Eventually the line linked up with Waterford in 1854, with the journey terminating at Sallypark. Ten years later, the Waterford and Limerick Railway with the Waterford and Kilkenny Railway line constructed a station built from handsome brick which resided by the riverside until 1966.

The Waterford–Limerick line had the fastest passenger trains on the island of Ireland. Its locomotives were manufactured by Kitson of Leeds and Dubbs in Glasgow, Scotland. Six of these locomotives endured until 1949 before being scrapped. This service was independent until it was taken over by the giant that was the Great Southern and Western Railway.

In 1872, the Waterford, Dungarvan and Lismore Railway commenced its building and was completed in 1878. This is testament to engineering ingenuity is matched by the marvel of the landscape within which it is situated. The line depended on the transportation of livestock and English travellers. In 1888, a Texan businessman staged a train crash as an attraction which brought a great crowd to the event, but tragically resulted in the death of eight people when a boiler exploded. A station at Bilberry in the city was in operation until 1908 before being used as a store for materials in the construction of Redmond Bridge. Yet one of the most notable dates in the history of this station was 2 May 1904. King Edward VII travelled from Lismore, with his train journey ending in Bilberry. The day also had added significance when the city's mayor, James Power, was knighted, and was the last Waterford man to receive such an honour from the English monarchy. The line was taken over by the Great Southern and Western in 1898. The service lasted until 1913.

The station was transformed into a munitions factory from 1917 to 1919 and remained closed until Allied Ironfounders began its operations there in 1935.

The Waterford, Kilkenny and Central Ireland Railway eventually established a terminus in the city in 1864 after the first section of the line (from Kilkenny to Thomastown) had opened in 1848. It offered people a direct route from Waterford to Dublin (though an earlier line from Kilkenny via Carlow had been in existence since 1844). The railway line is noteworthy for being the first to use locomotives with a side tank engine. This service carried 520,000 passengers and up to 28,000 tons of goods in 1865, despite passenger carriages being described as the poorest in the country. Such practices led to the decline of the line, which was then taken over by Great Southern and Western in 1900.

In 1853, the Waterford–Tramore railway remained an independent entity until being absorbed by the Great Southern Railway in 1925. It was instigated to link Waterford to Cork (via Youghal) in 1846. However, due to the difficulties that arose during the Famine, the Cork to Youghal section was built and the commencement of construction of the Waterford–Tramore began in 1851. Yet both lines were not linked up as originally planned. The line could

North Waterford Railway Station, *c.* 1900. *UK1655, Waterford County Museum*

Above left: Steam train, Manor Street Railway Station, Waterford, *c.* 1935. UK4025, *Waterford County Museum*

Above right: Manor Street Station on the Waterford–Tramore Railway line, 14 August 1953. UK4031, *Waterford County Museum*

boast having the world's oldest working locomotive in the 1930s. Sadly, on 24 August 1935 the train was derailed at Carricklong bridge, injuring the majority of crew and passengers. Nevertheless, there was only one other accident on the history of Waterford–Tramore railway line. On 14 August 1947, the train overshot its rails, landing by the De Luxe Hotel. One of the most prosperous lines in the country was closed in the 1960s.

The last railway to reach Waterford was the Dublin and South Eastern Railway which terminated at Ferrybank. Construction of the line began at Bray, County Wicklow, in 1847 and was not completed until 1904. Colloquially known as the 'Bloody Slow and Easy Railway' due to the speed of travel (but also apt in reference to its construction), it was subsumed by the Great Southern Railway in 1925.

VERE THOMAS ST LEGER GOOLD:
Wimbledon Finalist and Convicted Murderer

Born in Waterford on 2 October 1853, Goold became a keen player of lawn tennis in its early days in his native city, and became a member of Fitzwilliam Lawn Tennis Club in Dublin. In 1878, he won the men's singles event of the first Irish Open, which was held in Limerick. The following year the Irish Open was staged at his home club's courts, and he again won the men's singles title, receiving a prize of £20. His performance at the Irish Open that year saw Goold installed as the favourite for the Wimbledon championship held a week later. However, he was defeated in the final by Reverend John Hartley in front of over a thousand spectators. Unfortunately, this was to be not only Goold's only appearance in a Wimbledon final but also the tournament as a whole. Goold was considered an important member in the administration of the Fitzwilliam Lawn Tennis Club. His most notable tennis achievement until the end of his career in 1883 was winning a doubles match for Ireland against England in what has since been recognised as the first international tennis match between two nations. In 1886, Goold moved to London and met a Frenchwoman, Marie Violet (twice widowed), who he married in 1891.

Le Petit Journal, no. 875, 25 August 1907, St Leger Goold murder trial. He is the only Wimbledon finalist to have been convicted of murder.

After a brief period spent in Canada, they returned to London in 1903. However, an ill-fated foray into the laundry business led them to move to Monte Carlo, trying to achieve wealth through the gambling tables of casinos. On 6 August 1907, Goold and his wife were arrested after the discovery of a dismembered body of a woman, named Emma Liven, in their luggage. The trial revealed that Liven was murdered after trying to obtain repayment of a loan she had given Goold and his wife, and was struck when a heated argument erupted. As a result, Goold was imprisoned on Devil's Island, French

Guiana, and died a year later on 8 September 1909. His wife was imprisoned and died in 1914. Vere Goold holds the double distinction of being the first tennis player born on the island of Ireland to contest a Wimbledon final, and the only Wimbledon finalist to be convicted of murder.

WATERFORD'S PEOPLE'S PARK

… while this Park falls short in magnitude and appearance of many constructed for similar purposes in other parts of the kingdom, it is a source of pride that it is the only one in Ireland of a People's Park.

Lieutenant-Colonel Roberts' address on the opening of the People's Park, August 1857

Situated at the intersection of William Street and the Park Road, the People's Park was formed from the marshland which was known as Lombard's Marsh along Newtown Road. The creation of the park was ordered by the Mayor of Waterford, John A. Blake, in 1855 and led to St John's River being diverted again in 1857 and the marshland drained to create the 16.3-acre park. The gardener, Mr Nevin, produced the original design for the park. It was opened in August 1857 when staging the Royal Agricultural Show and completed in November of the same year.

Above left: People's Park, *c.* 1900. EB145, *Waterford County Museum*

Above right: People's Park, *c.* 1900. UK2137, *Waterford County Museum*

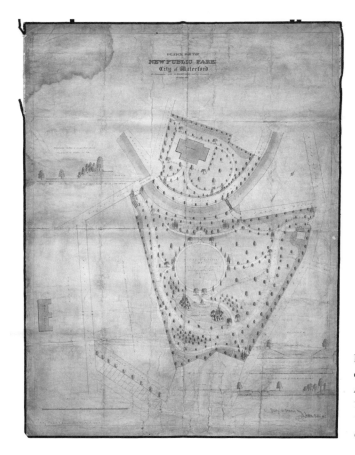

People's Park design by Alexander Nimmo 1855. *M-PL-2, Waterford City & County Archives*

Further developments to the People's Park include a Victorian bandstand which was erected in 1869 and the Goff cycle track dating to 1891. By the bandstand are two Russian guns which date to the Crimean War. An ornamental fountain was constructed in 1883 but was vandalised in 1977, and later again beyond repair in the 1980s. Today, a small fountain with a sphere is located where the original fountain once stood.

The old caretaker's residence is now the Park Lodge Café. There is a children's playground and skateboarding park, the latter of which was part of the refurbishment of the People's Park, which received €1 million in funding in 2006 for further development. The park is connected to the courthouse by an iron bridge.

CLOCK TOWER

The Clock Tower.

... the tower is a thing of beauty as well as of usefulness. Observe the fine quality of the stonework; the delicate spire; the diamond shapes and gothic pinnacles of the clock faces; the trefoil-headed recesses of the water stoups.

Julian Walton

The Clock Tower is one of Waterford City's most recognisable landmarks situated on the Quay. Designed by Charles Tarrant in the Gothic Revival style, it was constructed between 1854 to 1861. The tower performed an important function, as time was pivotal to the shipping industry which was in rude health in Waterford in the latter half of the nineteenth century. There are four cast-iron clock faces which look north, south, east and west. In addition, there are three drinking fountains, all of which are on the landward sides to provide fresh water for horses.

THE CLYDE SHIPPING COMPANY

The world's oldest steamship company began a weekly service to Cork and Waterford from Glasgow in 1859. Ships to have serviced this route were the *Killarney, Vivandiere, Wicklow* (1863) and *Rockabill* (1878). In partnership with the Malcolmson brothers, the Clyde operated services from Belfast to Plymouth, and from Waterford to London in 1870. Frank P. Murphy sees this as: 'the Clyde knew what they were up against and wisely co-operated rather than compete.' The fall of the Malcolmsons led Clyde to assume the Waterford Steamship Company in 1912.

The First World War was a difficult time for the Clyde Shipping Company. Several of its ships were torpedoed during the conflict. During the 1916 Easter Rising in Dublin, the *Coningbeg* entered Liverpool on

26 April but was requisitioned to transport British Army troops to combat the insurrection. The *Dunbrody* was also called into action in April of the following year, when under the guidance of Captain Spillane it successfully rescued fifty-seven horses aboard the *Hermione*, which was torpedoed but managed to get near the port. There was great tragedy in December 1917 when two of the Clyde's ships, the *Coningbeg* and *Formby*, were sunk by a German submarine (looked at in further detail later).

After the war, the steamers of the Clyde were primarily used to transport cattle between Waterford and Liverpool. The *Rockabill* was the last ship after the Second World War to continue this route.

JOHN WYSE POWER:
the Man who Gave the GAA its Name

Born at Knockhouse outside of Waterford City in 1859, John Wyse Power attended Mount Sion school and is suggested to have 'put love of country before personal advancement' by his old schoolmate Councillor McDonald of Waterford Corporation upon his death in 1926. It seems Wyse Power's association with Edmund Rice's school foreshadows the strong hurling tradition of Mount Sion in Waterford, both school and club, the latter of which was founded in 1932.

A career in the British administration in Ireland was curtailed by his simmering nationalist sympathies (he was a fluent Irish speaker) which led to a career in journalism, becoming the editor of the *Leinster Leader* in 1883. Wyse Power was also being monitored by British authorities for his connections to the Fenians and Irish Republican Brotherhood. Moreover, it is suggested that he could have become Chief Secretary of Ireland if not for the political career of William Edward Foster, known as 'Buckshot' for his apparent ordering of the police to fire on a crowd. Wyse Power was arrested and spent time in Naas Jail as one of 'Foster's Suspects'.

At Hayes Hotel in Thurles on 1 November 1884, he was one of the participants in the founding of the Gaelic Athletic Association (GAA). Furthermore, his role as one of the first secretaries of the association can be deemed to have set strong foundations that are still felt so vibrantly in twenty-first-century Ireland. Perhaps his position and Waterford connection were the factors in Tramore hosting the first All-Ireland championships three years later. His main interest was in the 'athletic' pursuits of the association more so than hurling and Gaelic football. Though a fervent nationalist, Wyse Power would resign his role as an assistant secretary in 1887 as a result of the banning of RIC members from the GAA. However, his association with Gaelic Games continued as the first chairman of the Dublin County Board. Furthermore, he would receive similar treatment to that of Michael Cusack by James Joyce, by also featuring in *Ulysses* as 'John Wyse Nolan'.

Politically, he aligned himself with the Land League, where he met his wife Jane 'Jennie' O'Toole. She was a founder member of the Sinn Fein Party of which she became vice president in 1912. In addition, she became one of the most important women of the revolution as president of Cumann na mBan, and opposing the Anglo-Irish Treaty of 1921. They married around the same time as Wyse Power became editor of the *Leinster Leader* in Naas. Two years later he became a staff member of the *Freeman's Journal* and later editor of the *Evening Herald* during the height of Parnellism in Ireland.

He died on 29 May 1926, survived by his wife (now a senator of the fledgling Irish Free State), his son Charles (named after Parnell) a circuit judge for Galway and Mayo, and his daughter Dr Nancy Power, a travelling academic of Celtic studies. His tombstone was recently refurbished in Glasnevin Cemetery, while a plaque at the *Leinster Leader* commemorates his achievements. His role as a proponent of Irish nationalism as well as being one of the key figures in the establishment of the GAA should see him receive more attention and, more importantly, acknowledgement.

HANLEY'S PIPE FACTORY

From 1869 to the early 1930s, Messrs Hanley and Co., situated on John's Lane, Waterford, manufactured clay pipes which were exported to America, Great Britain and South Africa. The clay pipe was known as the 'Workman's pipe' and was still popularly used in Waterford when it declined across the country around 1917 as cigarettes became more fashionable. The owner of the factory, a Mr O'Neill, believed that those who smoked the clay pipe compared to cigarette smokers lived longer, as the clay absorbed a large amount of the nicotine from the tobacco.

THE JEWISH COMMUNITY IN WATERFORD

In 1701, Jacob Nunes was given the freedom of the city to trade by the Council of Waterford Corporation, which Louis Hyman states 'encouraged the settlement of foreign merchants'. By 1871, there was still only one Jewish person living in Waterford. Upon the instituting of the May Laws in Tsarist Russia, many Jews came to Britain and Ireland to evade persecution. Those that would come to Waterford resided at Manor Street. Many of them were originally from Wales, although they were known in Ireland as 'English Jews'. In 1893, a Jewish congregation had been formed in the city with its president being a Mr R. Smullian. This allowed members of the Jewish community in Waterford to practise their faith and perform rituals without having to travel to Belfast or Dublin where there were a more concentrated community and synagogues (established in Waterford at No. 88 the Manor).

The first Jewish wedding took place on 14 November 1894, the couple being a Mr Jack Lappin and a Miss Fanny Diamond. The ceremony attracted great interest, with many Christians in attendance. Such was the growth of the Jewish community that the creation of a Hebrew School was planned in 1896. They became further involved in Irish society, such as in the world of politics. In 1905, Harris Sherowitz sent correspondence to Irish Parliamentary Party leader John Redmond seeking amendments to the Aliens Act. The 1911 census saw the figure for Jews in Waterford reach 62. Furthermore, by the 1930s, a Maurice Woolfson played an integral part in foreshadowing the Factory Leagues (soccer) in the city.

GENERAL POST OFFICE

The construction of the General Post Office, located on the Quay, began in 1875, undertaken by local builder James Ryan. The site of the GPO was previously occupied by the old Custom House as well as the original offices of the Clyde Shipping Company. An additional extension had to be erected to cater for the growing parcel and telegraph services. The *National Inventory of Architectural Heritage* appraises that the GPO is 'an imposing civic and commercial building in a striking Venetian Gothic style, which is an unusual feature in the streetscape of Custom House Quay'.

WATERFORD CITY TRAMWAY:
the Tram That Never Was

Midway through the nineteenth century, the Waterford Corporation surmised that the future development of the city would occur at its western side (the area now known as Gracedieu). The corporation believed that central to aiding such a development was having a sufficient public transport service. As already outlined, there was substantial growth in railway service across Ireland and in Waterford City. In January 1878, it was agreed that a horse-drawn tramway be established with the construction of a double line tramway from Gilbert Hill (Gracedieu) to Adelphi Quay in the city centre.

The following month, the Harbour Commissioners made a submission to the council proposing that a tramway be developed connecting the railway system south of the River Suir to the port to aid trade. However, the corporation were not willing to give any concrete promises to what appeared to be a lucrative idea. Albert Thornton notes that:

> The proposed tramway was based on the premise that the Waterford, Dungarvan and Lismore Railway Company would provide a connection with the main railway network, by the construction of an extension railway from Waterford South Railway Station at Bilberry (Waterford Foundry Ltd), to a new city centre terminus at the junction of Bridge St. and Mary St.

The line would be built behind the existing brewery with a tunnel through Bilberry Rock (at three furlongs, nine chains and fifty links) and was given the go-ahead after an Act of Parliament for the development was passed on 22 July 1878. However, the line was never built, which subsequently hampered any future development of a tramway service in the city. This was

FREEDOM OF WATERFORD CITY

From 1876, Irish cities had the right to create Honorary Freedom under the Municipal Privilege Act. Below is a list of those who received this honour from Waterford Corporation since the introduction of the act. The majority of the list was compiled originally through the research and efforts of former Waterford City archivist Donal Moore.

ADMITTED AS HONORARY FREEMEN OF WATERFORD CITY SINCE 1876:

Issac Butt	6 February 1876	'… in recognition of services rendered … in restoring to this corporation the privilege of nominating the gentlemen to act as High Sheriff of this ancient municipality'.
Charles Stewart Parnell	6 December 1880	'… in recognition of his eminent services in the cause of Ireland …'
John Dillon	1 November 1881	Dillon was a supporter of land reform and Irish Home Rule.
William O'Brien	15 November 1887	MP. '… now a prisoner in Tullamore Gaol'. '… we consider their [the British Government] conduct in depriving him of his clothing as meriting the contempt of the human race'.
T.D. Sullivan	2 January 1888	MP, Lord Mayor of Dublin. '… in recognition of his eminent service in the cause of Ireland'.
Gen. F.S. Roberts	28 August 1893	MP, Lord Mayor of Dublin. '… in recognition of his eminent service in the cause of Ireland'.
John Redmond	12 September 1902	MP for Waterford City since 1891 until his death in 1918.
Andrew Carnegie	19 October 1903	On occasion of laying of foundation stone for Carnegie Library

E. O'Meagher Condon	29 September 1909	One of the five people charged at the time of the Manchester martyrs, he spent 12 years in prison.
Richard R. Cherry	7 December 1909	Lord Justice of Appeal. '... whose early association with our City, whose Parliamentary ability and success and whose final elevation to the supreme Tribunal in Ireland are such characteristics as warrant us in giving to him the franchise of our County Borough'.
Archbishop Daniel Mannix	12 August 1925	'... In recognition of his indomitable stand in defence of the democratic principle of free and unfettered government'. Freedom was proposed on 17/8/1920.
Most Rev. Dr Paschal Robinson	15 May 1930	First Papal Nuncio to visit city since seventeenth century.
Eamon de Valera	28 January 1946	Taoiseach.
Sean T. O Ceallaigh	30 May 1955	President of Ireland.
Fr Augustine Sepinski, O.F.M.	15 April 1957	Minister General, Franciscan Order on the occasion of the unveiling of the statue of Luke Wadding, O.F.M.
Michael Cardinal Browne, O.P.	7 August 1962	Native of Waterford City.
William Cardinal Conway	28 May 1966	Primate of All-Ireland.
William F. Watt	26 May 1969	Businessman and founder of Waterford Music Club.
Rt Rev. Charles J. Henderson	6 April 1973	Native of Waterford. Bishop of Tricola.
Patrick W. McGrath	8 June 1973	Chairman of Waterford Crystal.
John Treacy	25 July 1979	Winner of two World Cross-Country titles.
Rev. Bro. Gerard G. McHugh, C.F.C.	24 August 1979	Superior General of the Congregation of Christian Brothers. On the occasion of the translation of the remains of Bro. Rice to the Blessed Sacrament Chapel, Mount Sion.

John W. Armstrong	14 August 1980	Church of Ireland Archbishop and Primate.
Noel M. Griffin	24 November 1980	Former managing director of Waterford Crystal.
Matthias Barrett	18 January 1981	Waterford native. Founder of Little Brothers of the Good Shepherd.
Seán Kelly	23 January 1987	'A Waterford man who has the achieved the position of No.1 cyclist in the world.'
Bro. Felan Burns	23 October 1987	'Provincial of De La Salle Brothers. On occasion of the centenary of the Order in the city.'
Mrs Mary Robinson	1 July 1994	President of Ireland.
Michael Doody	9 February 1996	Waterford native. Former City Manager.
Anna Manahan	19 April 2002	'In recognition of her contribution to world theatre and for being an ambassador for Waterford.' Actress, Waterford native. Winner of 'Tony' award on Broadway, NY, for Best Featured Actress, 1998.
Nicholas Fewer	2006	'… tremendous work for the city down through the years, whether it be in his own profession; in his driving of the Strategy Waterford group; as chairman of the regional airport or – most recently – as chairman of the team that organised the city's memorable hosting of the Tall Ships Races' [in 2005].
Brendan Bowyer	17 June 2011	In respect of their careers in the music and entertainment industry which 'talents and creativity have allowed them span the years'.
Val Doonican	17 June 2011	

GAEILGEOIRÍ IN THE CITY

The Census figures for 1881 show that a mere seven people spoke only Irish in Waterford City. This figure would remain the same ten years later but would increase to twenty-four in 1901. One commentator in *Decies* journal from October 1976 wryly suggests, 'One possibility is that some Gaelic League enthusiasts went so far as to "forget" their English completely when Her Majesty's census enumerators called.'

HEAVYWEIGHT BOXING:
Champion of the World Visits Waterford, December 1887

John L. Sullivan, 'The champion of champions', 1898. Sullivan was the last heavyweight champion of bare-knuckle boxing under London Prize Ring Rules and the first heavyweight champion of gloved boxing. *Library of Congress*

The last bare-knuckle boxing champion of the world was Irish-American John L. Sullivan. He formed the link between the old style and modern boxing under the Queensberry Rules. While still heavyweight champion of the world, Sullivan toured Ireland in 1887. On Tuesday, 13 December 1887, he departed Dublin for Waterford on the nine o'clock train. At each stop on the journey he received a warm reception and it is believed that he had time to visit Donnelly's Hollow, a natural amphitheatre in County Kildare where Dan Donnelly defeated Englishman George Cooper in 1815.

Hundreds gathered along the Quay to get a glimpse of the 'Boston Strong Boy' as he made his way to the Imperial Hotel (now the Tower Hotel). That evening, Sullivan sparred with his sidekick Jack Ashton in an exhibition at the Theatre Royal. The *Freeman's Journal* noted that 'whilst the men were on stage the spectators seemed to be simply spellbound'.

After the sparring session, Sullivan spoke to the crowd that his trip across the Atlantic had originally been to allow him to fight the English champion Jem Smith, but now he had to settle for a bout with Charlie Mitchell, though he remarked to the crowd that it didn't matter who he fought. Sullivan was to leave Waterford for Cork the next day to fight local amateur Frank Creedon.

PURCELL O'GORMAN:
'The Joker for Waterford'

Purcell O'Gorman was born in Dublin in 1820 and was an army officer and later a Home Rule MP for Waterford City from 1874 to 1880. Considered a humourist in Westminster, Benjamin Disraeli advised MPs who were gloomy to cheer themselves up by witnessing O'Gorman's speeches. In the 13 March 1875 issue of *Vanity Fair,* there was a cartoon of the Waterford City MP by 'Ape' with the caption 'The Joker for Waterford'. Upon his death in November 1888, O'Gorman's obituary in the *Irish Times* stated that he:

always left the hearer doubtful whether the bull was not intended and the blunder deliberate and whether the big Irishman was laughing in his sleeve at the legislature, which thought it was laughing at him… when the signal flew along the line 'O'Gorman is up', the diner dropped his fork, the bibber his grog, the smoker his cigar, and from dining-room, smoke-room and bar the crowd came packing.

He was a larger-than-life character who certainly was one of the more eccentric representatives for the city at the Imperial parliament at Westminster.

Purcell O'Gorman, *Vanity Fair,* 13 March 1875.

WATERFORD CORPORATION'S HOUSING PROGRAMME SINCE 1879

YEAR	STREET	HOUSES BUILT
1879	Green Street	17
1887	Summerhill Terrace	25
1887/9	Presentation Row	18
	Cannon Street	8
	Slievekeale Road	9
	Emmet Place	26
	Newport's Lane	10
	Grange Terrace	17
1898	Monastery Street	9
	Mount Sion Avenue	36
1899	St Ignatius Street	20
1900	Morrisson's Road	24
	Barrack Street	21
	Doyle's Street	24
1910	Morrisson's Road	17
	Monastery Street	16
	Alexander Street	14
	Doyle Street	12
1910/11	Mount Sion Avenue	36
1915	Doyle Street	14
	Upper Yellow Road	10
1915/17	Trinity Square	38
1922	Morrisson's Road	20
	Griffith Place	20
1923	Slievekeale	6
1932	Upper Yellow Road	8
	Congress Place	73
	Morrisson's Road	2
	Ozanam Street	14
1933	Morrisson's Road	21
	Morrisson's Avenue	24
	Dominic Place	110

1934	Lower Yellow Road	6
	Philip Street	8
1935	Upper Yellow Road	22
	Morrisson's Avenue	40
	Keane's Road	25
	Tycor Avenue	35
	Ard na Greine	9
	Sexton Street	9
	Newport's Lane	14
1936	Keane's Road	11
	Griffith Place	42
	Ard na Greine	50
	Tycor Avenue	8
	Slievekeale Road	14
	Luke Wadding Street	2
	Sexton Street	20
	Morrisson's Avenue	8
	Leamy Street	24
1937	Hennessy's Road	36
	Blake's Lane	2
	Prior's Knock	32
1938	Poleberry/Poleberry Terrace	13
	Barrack Street Terrace	12
	St Carthages Avenue	16
1941	Cannon Street	46
	Prior's Knock	34
1948	Pearse Park	46
1949	Cork Road	168
	Hennessy's Road	37
1951	Cannon Street Terrace	13
	Bernard Place	10
	Congress Place	4
	Ozanam Street	4
	Morrisson's Avenue	2
	Roanmore Park	76
	Prior's Knock	22
	Hennessy's Road	24
1951/53	Rockenham	125

1953/58/63	St John's Park	432
1954	Mount Sion Avenue	40
1957	Newport's Square	30
1958/59	Lower Yellow Road	6
	Newport's Lane	10
1959	Carrigeen Park	10
1961/62	Blake's Lane	33
1963	Cathal Brugha Street	37
1965/66	Rice Park/College Road	73
1966	Kingsmeadow	90
1967/68	St Killian's Place	33
1968/70	Lisduggan	331
1973	Tigeens, Kilbarry	6
1973/74	Larchville	286
1974	St Killian's Place	21
1974/76	Ballybeg	223
1977/78	Priory Lawn	131
1979/82	Clonard Park	215
1980	Ballytruckle Court	9
	Passage Road	10
1981	Belmont Heights	47
	Butchers Lane/Barrack Street	11
	Lower Grange	10
1983	Wilkin Street and Court	20
	Upper Yellow Road	10
	Rockshire Road	25
	Francis Court	
	Larchville (OPD's)	15
	Ardmore Park, Ballybeg	96
1984	Francis Street	3
1984/85	Kilcohan Park	129
1985	Upper Grange – Farran Park	76
	Ballytruckle Green	43
	Costelloe's Lane	
	Barrett Place	21

1986	Ardmore Park, Ballybeg	61
1987	Closegate	56
	Barrett Court / Doyle Street	22
	Walter Street / Lower Newtown	27
1987/88	St Herblain Park	105

'THE UNIQUENESS OF BALLYBRICKEN THAT UNDERWROTE THE DURABILITY OF REDMONDISM':
The Pig Buyers' Strike, 1890s

The Pig Buyers' Association at Ballybricken was recognised by John Redmond, MP for Waterford City and subsequently leader of the Irish Home Rule Movement from 1900–18, for its 'patriotism and sterling spirit' in his electioneering in the 1890s. A trade disagreement between the pig buyers and the bacon curers, who sought to buy directly from farmers therefore cutting out the middleman, the pig buyers, led to an economic blockade with violence unleashed by the members of its association. Farmers seeking to sell to the bacon curers, such as Denny's and Shaw's in Waterford City, had to be escorted by police. This led to the deployment of 155 R.I.C. Officers which amounted to 'almost one for every pig buyer'.

The bacon factories in the city employed over 800 people at this time and the pig buyers sought to preserve their livelihood, which was under threat and compounded by competition from Denmark and restrictions abroad such as a constraint on imported pork products in Germany. The pig buyers were able to gain the support of dockers who declined to transport a cargo of salt for Richardsons aboard the ship *Yarra Yarra*. The pig buyers also refused to frequent public houses or restaurants which served produce from farmers who didn't go through them. Tensions would see fifteen salters from the Denny's factory attacked by a mob of an estimated 200 men.

John Redmond played a pivotal role in bringing the dispute to an end. He represented the pig buyers in court and gained favourable terms for the association, effectively returning the system of trade to its previous state. Waterford labour historian Emmet O'Connor concludes that the result of the strike not only weakened the cause of trade unionism but strengthened 'working class conservatism' that formed 'the uniqueness of Ballybricken that underwrote the durability of Redmondism'. It was a political philosophy that continued into the twentieth century.

JOHN REDMOND:
Leader of the Home Rule Movement

Born in Wexford to a Catholic gentry family, his mother was a Protestant unionist from Wicklow. The family name was synonymous with the politics of the county, with both his great-uncle and father being its representatives in the Imperial Parliament in Westminster. Described as an 'unexceptional student' at Trinity College Dublin after first attending Clongowes, his time at Trinity should be noted for the reason that it was unusual for a Catholic to attend it in the nineteenth century. After serving as a clerk in the vote office at Westminster he took his father's seat and became the party whip of the Irish nationalist grouping.

Tours of the British colonies of Australia and New Zealand strengthened his 'lifelong belief that Ireland should play a full role in developing the empire'. This conviction in empire stemmed from seeing it as what David Fitzpatrick would term 'an instrument of civilisation and progress' that could further the cause of Irish independence rather than hamper it. The role of the Irish in the creation and expansion of the British Empire led Redmond to essentially see the 'Irish Question' from an English perspective. In addition, the wife of William O'Brien, Sophie, wrote that it was Redmond's 'cool manner that impressed Englishmen, as being so unlike an Irishman's'. From this, John Redmond attempted to sanitise the raw emotional nature that governed Irish nationalism previously, with the rationale that complete separation from Britain would mean the loss of sharing in the trappings of its Commonwealth, which would in turn be averse to the progress of an Irish nation.

His continued loyalty to Charles Stewart Parnell in the early 1890s saw him vacate his own Wexford seat to contest his former leader's constituency of Cork City after his death. Humiliation followed, with Redmond receiving less than a third of the vote. However, by chance of circumstance, a few weeks later Redmond recorded a remarkable victory over Michael Davitt of Land League fame in Waterford City, the first of a number of instances where the city by the River Suir was different from the rest of nationalist Ireland by returning a Parnellite. Though the fickle nature of people is wryly outlined by Sophie O'Brien, it was women who were the 'fiercest Parnellites', as his fall was the result of his love for Katherine O'Shea rather than the cause of Ireland.

The seat remained with Redmond until his death in 1918. He was succeeded by his son William Archer, while the rest of southern Ireland apparently shifted to Sinn Fein in 1918. He united the Irish Party and became its leader in 1900. Redmond was an influential figure at the Land Conference of 1902 which led to the creation of the Land Act of 1903, which aided tenant land purchase. He was involved in negotiations which concluded with the establishment of the National University in 1908. Redmond secured the introduction of the third Home Rule Bill in 1912, which was postponed due to the outbreak of the First World War in 1914. He encouraged members of the National Volunteers to join the British Army and fight in the war in defence of the liberty of small nations.

The 1916 Easter Rising would alter nationalist political perceptions, and Redmond was unable to recover any political momentum. He died suddenly on 6 March 1918.

NOTEWORTHY PERSONALITIES BORN IN WATERFORD IN THE NINETEENTH CENTURY

PATRICK O'KEEFE: SURVIVOR OF THE RMS *TITANIC*

Born in 1890, Patrick O'Keefe, who lived in 2 Spring Garden, Waterford City, boarded the *Titanic* at Queenstown aged 22 after a month's holiday. Originally to return on the *Baltic*, O'Keefe's brother persuaded him to stay and enjoy the Easter holidays in Ireland. It is believed that O'Keefe first came to America in 1904 aged 13. Having made several trips home to Ireland over the years, he worked as a hotel porter in New York. It is reported that he was very apprehensive of his return trip after having a premonition of the ominous fate that awaited the *Titanic*. He travelled alone as a third-class passenger, and remained aboard the ship until its sinking, when he and several passengers and crew managed to avoid going down with the ship by untying Collapsible B. The raft became infamous as it was turned upside down, and thirty survivors were rescued the following morning. It was a number of weeks before Patrick O'Keefe returned to work, needing time to recover from his injuries. He was one of only sixty-nine men out of 500 from third class who survived the disaster. He continued to work as a hotel porter in New York, and married Ann Nolan in September 1923. They had two children. He died aged 48 in 1939, plagued by the disaster of the 'unsinkable' *Titanic*.

D.P. MORAN: NATIONALIST AND GAELIC LEAGUE ADVOCATE

Daniel Patrick Moran was an editor and phrasemaker born in Waterford in 1896. Educated at Castleknock near Dublin, Moran worked as a journalist in London and later returned to Ireland, and became a vociferous nationalist and advocate of the Gaelic League. His journal, the *Leader*, established in 1900 (published until 1971), criticised any features of Irish life which were not Catholic or Gaelic. D.P. Moran labelled Protestants as 'sour-faces', the Anglo-Irish as 'West Britons' and those who copied English mannerisms as 'Shoneens'. He coined the phrase 'Irish Ireland' in a series of articles published in *The Philosophy of Irish Nationalism* (1905). Moran died in Sutton, Dublin in 1936.

THE WILD MAN FROM BORNEO:
Grand National Winner 1895

The Widger family in Waterford were horse-breeders who supplied horses to cavalry regiments across Europe, primarily in England, Italy and the Netherlands. Joe Widger had an ambition to have success in the horse racing industry, and rode his first winner aged 13 at Bangor. He and his brother John bought a horse named *The Wild Man from Borneo* (so-called after two well-known stuntmen) in 1893 with a view to competing at the Grand National at Aintree in the following year. On his first run in the hardest race in the National Hunt, he came third having taking the lead at the penultimate fence.

The Widgers and *The Wild Man from Borneo* were back at Aintree in 1895 with Joe Widger guiding the horse to contention coming up onto the last fence. Under his guidance *The Wild Man from Borneo* won the race by one and a half lengths, with celebrations aplenty in their hometown. The horse would compete two more times in the Grand National in 1896 and 1897 and was pulled up in the latter race.

CATHERINE STREET:
the Birthplace of Irish Motoring

In 1900, William Peare and Sir William Goff opened Ireland's first motor garage in Waterford City. The pair opened a brand new, state-of-the-art premises in Catherine Street with two storeys; the upper floor was a space for offices and accommodation, and the ground floor acted as a workshop and showroom. Peare began to sell Gladiator cars from 1902, and later acquired the rights as an agent for Daimler, Oldsmobile, Napier, Buick and Cadillac. Sadly, the garage closed in 1917, as William Peare decided to join the army and fight in the First World War. Goff's role in the whole enterprise led to his Napier being the first registered car in Waterford with its registration number reading WI–I.

An array of Morris cars on the forecourt of John Kelly's garage at Catherine Street, 18 December 1928. *Poole Collection, WP 3600, National Library of Ireland*

WATERFORD CITY LIBRARY

At the heart of Waterford City, the library has traditionally been regarded as a library for the people.

Jane Cantwell, Waterford City Librarian.

Waterford City Library was designed by Albert Edward Murray, located on a site donated by Mayor Alexander Nelson. It is one of five libraries in County Waterford sponsored by the philanthropist Andrew Carnegie and is apparently his first contribution towards the building of libraries in Ireland. Classical in style, the Carnegie Library was built from limestone ashlar in 1903. Refurbished in the early twenty-first century, the library now inhabits Lady Lane and Bakehouse Lane in the city centre. During excavations prior to the restoration and extension of the library, part of the old City Wall was uncovered. It reopened to the public on 12 January 2004.

Waterford City, c. 1900. UK2878, Waterford County Museum

7

FROM HERE TO MODERNITY:
Twentieth-Century Waterford

TIMELINE

1915 CE: The opening of the Coliseum occurs on 18 October with a cabaret show. The following day, *Fatal Legacy* is the first film shown in the cinema.

1916 CE: Patrick Pearse speaks at the Town Hall on 10 February.

1921 CE: For the first time, women are permitted to make up juries.

1922 CE: On 18 July, the Siege of Waterford begins, with the army of the Irish Free State attacking the Anti-Treaty IRA posts in the city. The siege ends on 21 July.

1923 CE: A soviet is declared at the gasworks on the waterside on 22 January. A red flag is raised over the gasworks by striking workers over a dispute over the trimming of coal by the ITGWU and the Dockers Union. On 10 March, the gasworks soviet ends when the army moves in and removes workers from the site. Later that year, Caitlín Brugha is elected Waterford's first female TD.

1924 CE: The Waterford and District Football League is established.

1926 CE: Kathleen Phelan becomes Waterford's first female barrister.

1929 CE: The Theatre Royal shows the first talking film in Waterford, which is *The Singing Fool* with Al Jolson starring.

1943 CE: On 4 March, a section of the wall of Ballybricken Jail collapses leading to the deaths of ten people.

1947 CE: Construction begins of the Waterford Glass Factory at Kilcohan.

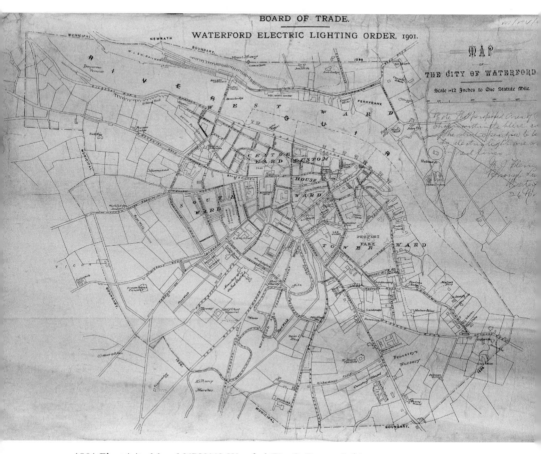

1901 Electricity Map. *M/PV/43, Waterford City & County Archives*

1948 CE: Waterford wins its first senior All-Ireland hurling title, defeating Dublin by 6–7 to 4–2.

1949 CE: In February, the demolition of Ballybricken Jail begins. The building of Airmount Maternity Hospital commences on 26 April.

1952 CE: Ardkeen Hospital opens as a Tuberculosis Sanatorium on 21 June before becoming a General Hospital in 1958.

1959 CE: The Waterford International Light Opera Festival is first held. On 4 October, Waterford wins its second senior All-Ireland hurling title, defeating Kilkenny by 3–12 to 1–10.

From Here to Modernity: Twentieth-Century Waterford

1960 CE: The Waterford to Tramore Railway closes on 3 December.

1962 CE: Waterford's first set of traffic lights come into operation at the Carstand.

1965 CE: The first phase of Rice Park housing scheme is completed.

1966 CE: The ferry service from Waterford to Liverpool closes, with the last voyage of the *Great Western* on 24 December.

1967 CE: Waterford Industrial Estate opens in July, with the first factory being the pharmaceutical company Hadensa.

1968 CE: The 331 houses that comprise Lisduggan housing estate are completed.

1971 CE: At Ardkeen Services Garage, Waterford's first fully automatic coin-operated carwash begins working.

1972 CE: The Denny's Bacon Factory closes on 3 March with the loss of 240 jobs.

1973 CE: Larchville housing scheme is completed with the construction of 286 houses.

1974 CE: A four-day strike at the Waterford Glass Factory occurs in February. In March, the Ballybeg housing estate is opened. On 20 December, Goodbody's Jute Factory closes with the loss of 520 jobs.

1978 CE: Job losses at the National Board and Paper Mills in Grannagh and other factory closures lead to a protest over the haemorrhaging of jobs in Waterford with 20,000 people marching on 8 September. Hearne's Drapers on the Quay closes in November. The Munster Chipboard Factory closes in November 1979 and the National Board and Paper Mills close in September 1980.

1984 CE: On 22 October, the first phase of Rice Bridge is opened, with construction for the project costing £7.9 million. 30 November sees the closure of Clover Meats.

1985 CE: On 5 July, the first scheduled flight from a non-state airport in Ireland occurs at Waterford Regional Airport, operated by Ryanair, with the destination Gatwick Airport.

1987 CE: As part of the centralisation of services at Ardkeen Hospital, the County and City Infirmary closes on 31 October.

1989 CE: Waterford Local Radio receives the franchise for public broadcasting in Waterford and goes on air on 8 September.

1994 CE: On 1 July, the President of Ireland, Mary Robinson, is the first woman to receive the freedom of the city. In November, a royal charter granted to Waterford Chamber of Commerce is found in the vault of Bank of Ireland in the city. The document dates to 1815.

1995 CE: Airmount Maternity Hospital closes in July.

1997 CE: It is announced by Minister for Education, Niamh Breathnach, that Waterford Regional Technical College will be upgraded to an Institute of Technology. The Central Statistics Office releases figures that show Waterford City has the highest unemployment rate outside of the capital, with 12.65 per cent.

The city has a noble position along its mile of quay, and there is a good hotel, the Imperial, at the end of the broad and dignified Mall which leads down to the quay.

Stephen Gwynn, *The Charm of Ireland*, 1934.

A leading historian has stated that geography governs history. Waterford helps prove the point and the portents are positive. Its location has always been at the business end of our overseas affairs. Ireland being a small and relatively remote island, access is vital. Since Irish history began Waterford Harbour has been pivotal to events shaping its early and medieval fortunes. Now, with Ireland's future bound more closely with mainland Europe, Waterford could not be in a better position. If the historian is right we are in pole position and the future – and thereby potential – is bright … a fresher spirit abounds in contemporary Waterford underpinned by a feeling that there will be success. We have in the past indulged in whipping ourselves with what might have been and look what others have achieved and casting blame all over the place. Now, there is more a feeling of determination to realise potential by persistent effort. There is no other way – geography will govern our future story only if we help it. We are well located – let's make sure we become well connected and in every sphere of local activity. Success will depend on us all – the blame game is over.

Anthony Brophy, 'How are we doing?', *Munster Express*, 1999.

WATERFORD CITY IN THE IRISH REVOLUTIONARY DECADE

The introduction of the Home Rule Bill laws were delayed due to the outbreak of the First World War. John Redmond encouraged Irishmen to join in the fight for the freedom of small nations. Prior to 1916, 1,756 men from Waterford City enlisted, with 366 fatalities. The number of the inhabitants of the city around this time was 27,464 people. There were a higher number of recruits from the city compared with County Waterford, in part due to Redmond's support of the war. A recruiting office was established at Parnell Street and after the first four days 251 men had been recruited. The MP for the city, John Redmond, was influential in the high recruitment rate in the city and noted in December 1915 that 'Waterford has done its duty magnificently'.

View of Munition Factory, Waterford, 5 April 1917. *Poole Collection, IMP 1675, National Library of Ireland*

Economically, the city prospered due to the war, with an increase in the export of cattle, greater demand for bacon, and the establishment of a munitions factory which led to a state of near full employment. Hearne and Co. in the city received a contract to manufacture ammunition boxes in January 1915. The same business converted the South Station to an armaments factory in 1917, employing nearly 500 people, the vast majority of whom were women.

WATERFORD'S WAR DEAD:
John Condon and the Collins Brothers

The commemoration of the war has been contentious in Ireland after the partition of the island, with the historian Tom Hunt surmising that 'Ireland's commemoration of its war dead has always been compromised; at the war's end the country was on the verge of a revolution and those who returned from war came back to a very different country.'

The 1916 Easter Rising saw a political sea change across the majority of southern Ireland. A litmus test for the constituency took place in March 1918, when a by-election was held upon the death of John Redmond and won by his son Capt. Willie Redmond. The December general election for the same year saw Waterford as the only constituency outside of Belfast to return a Home Rule MP. This was a reflection of the loyalty to the legacy of John Redmond than of any political ideological demonstrations.

One of the tragic stories from the war was that of the Collins brothers from Balteen Lane (now Philip Street) in Waterford City. Of the six brothers who joined in the conflict, four of them died in Flanders or in the Somme, while a fifth went missing and was presumed dead but was later found badly wounded. The eldest brothers, Patrick and William, were career soldiers while the younger four siblings joined the army upon the outbreak of hostilities. The four brothers to die were Stephen (19 October 1914) and Michael (May 1915), both at Flanders; John died as a result of injuries from the Battle of the Somme (dying near Thiepval in Belgium on 9 September 1916) and Patrick on 29 March 1918. Joseph Christopher, known as Christy, was severely injured at Salonika and was presumed dead but was later repatriated to his native city.

Upon the death of Patrick, William was released from the army on compassionate grounds. He returned home to his mother and two younger siblings, Richard and Thomas, as their father had abandoned them during the war. His four brothers who died were aged from 16 to 30 years old. Rachel Collins, who researched the sad fate of these men, wrote in the *Irish Times*:

> I've never watched Saving Private Ryan. An aversion to violence, bloodshed and the sad inevitability of war means I haven't seen the epic … where Tom Hanks and his comrades face the carnage of the Normandy landings. Besides, the plot has always seemed a bit far-fetched. A family of boys wiped out by war; an army that was only too happy to send its sons to slaughter suddenly pulling out all the stops to save the last remaining brother.
>
> … while talking to my father, I learned that was not only such a story entirely plausible, it had played out in our family.

Another heart-breaking story from the First World War is of Private John Condon from Ballybricken who died at Bellevarde Ridge in the Second Battle of Ypres, Belgium, on 24 May 1915. His headstone records that he was 14 years old upon his death. Thus it was long believed that he was the youngest British soldier to die in the First World War. It is now known that he was 18 years old at the time of his death and was known as the 'Boy Soldier'. His grave at Poelkapelle Cemetery, Belgium, is much visited. Around 4,800 men from Waterford City and county fought in the First World War with over 1,100 dying in the hostilities.

DR MARY STRANGMAN:
Waterford Corporation's First Female Councillor

Born on 16 March 1872 to a Quaker family, Mary Strangman was the daughter of John Strangman, the founder of Strangman's Brewery in the city. She entered the Royal College of Surgeons, Dublin, in 1891, and after a time in England, set up her practice in 19 Parnell Street in 1902. She was a dynamic member of the Women's National Health Association (which she joined in 1908), an organisation that sought to reduce infant mortality and consumption. The enacting of the Local Authorities (Ireland) (Qualification of Women) Act in December 1911 allowed women to run for election for the first time. Dr Strangman ran and was elected for the Tower Ward for Waterford Corporation on 15 January 1912. In 1920, she vacated the seat and was chosen as the physician for Waterford City and County Infirmary. Dr Strangman was buried at the Quaker burial grounds at Newtown upon her death in 1943.

THOMAS ASHE:
Irish Patriot Educated at De La Salle

Thomas Ashe, the Irish revolutionary born and educated in Kinard, County Kerry, spent part of his education at De La Salle College, Waterford. He was a member of the Gaelic League, GAA, Irish Republican Brotherhood and commanded the Fingal Battalion of the Irish Volunteers. During the Easter Rising, Ashe's battalion captured the Rice House Barracks in Ashbourne, County Meath, resulting in the death of eleven Royal Irish Constabulary Officers. Ashe was sentenced to death for his role in the Rising, which was subsequently commuted to penal servitude for life. Released in June 1917, Ashe was re-imprisoned in August of the same year for giving a seditious speech in County Longford. Sentenced to two years' imprisonment, the former De La Salle student began a hunger strike with other Republican prisoners on 20 September in Mountjoy seeking to be recognised as prisoners of war. The strikers were forcibly fed, and on the fourth day of this practice Ashe collapsed and was brought to the Mater Hospital, where he was pronounced dead on 25 September 1917 due to heart and lung failure. His funeral took place in Dublin where it is believed 30,000 people attended. Michael Collins gave the oration at the funeral, saying, 'That volley which we have just heard is the only speech which it is proper to make over the grave of a dead Fenian.'

THE SINKING OF THE SS *FORMBY* AND *CONINGBEG*, DECEMBER 1917

These were steamboats of the 'Clyde Shipping Company.' The boats of this company ply on the cross-channel routes, Waterford to Liverpool, Bristol, Southampton, London, carrying mails, passengers, and general cargo, mostly agricultural produces. They are called 'Waterford boats', 'Clydeboats', and 'mail boats.'

It is customary on these crosschannel routes that when one ship is leaving here, her sister ship is leaving the port at the other side. Thus they generally meet in midchannel. The route, Waterford to Liverpool, takes about seventeen hours.

The Formby and the Coningbeg were on this route during the Great War.

Many of the crew of each were from Waterford Harbour district and the Hook.

One left Waterford: the other left Liverpool: there the story ends.

Charles Hearne in *The Schools' Collection*, Volume 0870, page 214, National Folklore Collection, University College Dublin.

Just ten days before Christmas Day 1917, the SS *Formby* and her sister ship the *Coningbeg* were torpedoed by a German submarine, U-62. In total eighty-three people perished aboard the vessels, sixty-seven of whom were from Waterford. In the service of the Clyde Shipping Company, both steamers serviced the Waterford to Liverpool route. The *Coningbeg* was the older of the two ships, built in 1904, belonging to the Waterford Steamship Company and named *Clodagh*. The *Formby* was built in 1914.

The master of U-62, Ernest Hashagen, in his memoirs describes the stalking of the *Coningbeg* as:

Monument to the *Coningbeg* and *Formby*.

> It is rather dreadful to be steaming thus alongside one's victim knowing that she has only ten or perhaps twenty minutes to live, till fiery death leaps from the sea and blows her to pieces. A solemn mood possesses the few upon the bridge. The horror of war silences us. Every one of our orders, every moment, every turn of a wheel is bringing death nearer our opponent. All is exactly settled in advance. We, too, have become part of fate.

Both ships had been held up in Liverpool due to bad weather. It seems that they were anxious to return home for Christmas. Only one body was ever recovered, that of stewardess Miss Annie O'Callaghan. Her remains washed up on St Brides Bay in Pembrokeshire where she was identified by her name on the back of a Sacred Heart badge which was pinned on her person. A message in a bottle washed up at Passage with the line '… we will never make the Hook' which is believed to have been connected to the sinking of the two vessels.

A local appeal fund was set up and raised almost £8,000 which provided some relief to relatives of the victims.

RICHARD MULCAHY:
The Irish Revolution's Unsung Hero and 'the Most Interesting Man in Europe'

Born in Waterford and educated at Mount Sion in the city, he later moved to Thurles and attended the local Christian Brothers' School. Mulcahy became an engineer in the Post Office in 1902. He would join the Gaelic League, the Irish Republican Brotherhood and the Irish Volunteers. He served as second-in-command to Thomas Ashe at the Battle of Ashbourne during the 1916 Easter Rising. After being interned at Knutsford and Frongoch, Mulcahy was released in November 1916 and was made Deputy Chief of Staff of the Volunteers working with Michael Collins.

As Chief of Staff of the Irish Republican Army, Mulcahy was elected to the first Dáil Éireann in 1919 and made Minister for Defence and later assistant to Cathal Brugha. D.J. Hickey and J.E. Doherty believe Mulcahy 'was largely responsible with Collins for directing the military struggle against Crown forces during the War of Independence'.

A supporter of the Anglo-Irish Treaty, Mulcahy was made Minister for National Defence in the Provisional Government while also serving as Chief of Staff of the army of the Irish Free State. He maintained communication with the anti-Treaty faction of the IRA and was a signatory of the army document which sought compromise between the opposing sides in the nationalist movement to maintain unity.

After the death of Michael Collins on 22 August 1922, Mulcahy was tasked with ending the Civil War, even meeting de Valera to bring an end to hostilities. A British journalist described Mulcahy as the 'most interesting man in Europe' in 1923. The article in *Colliers Magazine* went on to note that 'Michael Collins was the bold charging front of the rebellion: Mulcahy was the organising and planning brain.'

In March 1924, he resigned as Minister for Defence because of the Army Mutiny. He served as Minister for Local Government from 1927 to 1932. He was a founder member of the Fine Gael party and succeeded W.T. Cosgrave as party leader in 1944. In 1948, Mulcahy compromised with Clann na Poblachta in forming a government by allowing John A. Costello to become Taoiseach instead of himself as leader of the party. In this first Inter-Party government he served as Minister for Education from 1948 to 1951. In the second Inter-Party government he again did not become Taoiseach but served as Minister for the Gaeltacht from July to October 1956. He retired from parliament in 1961.

WATERFORD CITY AND THE WAR OF INDEPENDENCE

During the War of Independence, which took place from 1919 to 1921, the East Waterford Brigade of the Irish Republican Army was one of the most inactive units of the IRA on the island during the conflict. In the area of the East Brigade, one civilian, two members of the Royal Irish Constabulary and four members of the IRA died during the conflict. The East Brigade was led by Sean Matthews and covered the areas of Ballyduff, Dunhill, Gaultier and Waterford City. Some notable offences included an attack on Kill Royal Irish Constabulary Barrack in September 1920 and the Pickardstown Ambush, which saw the local IRA battalion suffer two fatalities, with Michael Wyley and Nicholas Whittle seriously wounded. It was a disastrous attempt to ambush a relieving military company to then attack the Tramore Barrack.

THE SIEGE OF WATERFORD, JULY 1922

The Siege of Waterford is referenced as the key event of the Civil War in Waterford, but to describe the events that took place as a siege is to be generous.

Tom Hunt, *The Little Book of Waterford* (2017)

The outbreak of civil war in 1922 upon the ratification of the Anglo-Irish Treaty saw Pax Whelan lead 300 members of the anti-Treaty IRA, also known as Irregulars, to seize prominent public buildings such as the Artillery

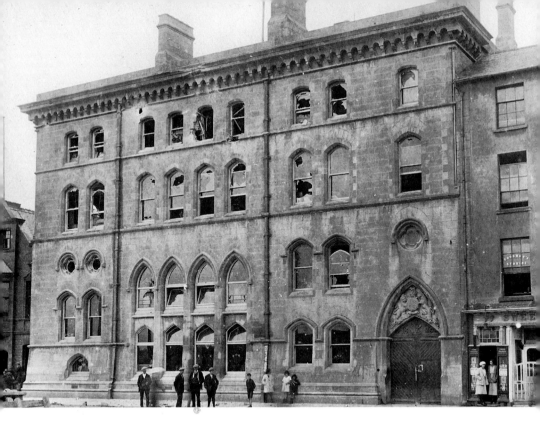

General Post Office, Waterford, after bombardment in 1922. *UK4072, Waterford County Museum*

Barrack, the General Post Office, the Granville Hotel, the Jail and Reginald's Tower. In addition, Redmond Bridge was raised to impede the ease of crossing the river. The Irregulars possessed rifles, revolvers and a small number of Thompson sub-machine guns.

The forces of the Irish Free State sought to regain control of the city, which started the siege of Waterford. The Free State army was led by Commandant-General John T. Prout and aided by Commandants Heaslip and Paddy Paul – the latter formerly commanded the East Waterford Brigade during the War of Independence – who were based on Mount Misery overlooking the city. They advanced from Kilkenny to the city on 14 July.

The Free State forces launched an attack with a single 18-pounder field gun. They made it to the city on 18 July, commencing the siege. Fire was exchanged with the occupied Artillery and Infantry Barrack coming under fire from the Free State army. Two days later the state forces crossed the River Suir 3 miles downriver from the city and reached its outskirts. Just after midnight they took the County Club and Adelphi Hotel without a single shot being fired. Reginald's Tower and the Imperial Hotel were no longer occupied by the Irregular IRA.

There was an exchange of fire at the General Post Office, with the Free State firing from the North Quay. The anti-Treaty faction moved from there to the Granville Hotel, with the last stand coming at the jail. The four-day siege ended with the Free State retaking the city while the Irregulars retreated westwards. The historian Michael Hopkinson concludes that '[e]ven by the standards of the Civil War the fall of Waterford demonstrated an extreme unwillingness on the part of the Republicans to fight and a complete failure of co-operation between anti-Treaty forces'.

WATERFORD SOVIET, APRIL 1920

The Irish Labour Party and Trade Union Congress called for a 24-hour general strike to be held on Tuesday, 13 April 1920. This was in response to sixty-six republican prisoners who were on hunger strike in Mountjoy, detained without charge, who sought status as political prisoners. This followed the anti-conscription strike in 1918 and a May Day one in 1919.

Luke Larkin, president of Waterford Workers' Council, brought a group made up of labour activists to City Hall seeking support from the Sinn Fein-controlled council. The day of the strike saw a march from City Hall to the cathedral followed by pickets which went to various hostelries to see that the strike was being observed. Later that night it was decided nationally that the strike was to continue indefinitely. The Wednesday saw skirmishes between Redmondites and strikers at Ballybricken. After 5 o'clock, the British authorities had reversed their stance on the hunger strikers in Mountjoy. In response, a red flag was raised above City Hall in Waterford with Luke Larkin speaking to the gathered crowd:

> Fellow comrades, this manifestation of Labour's power makes epoch [sic] in the history of the working classes … the cause of Labour is the cause of Ireland and the cause of Ireland is the cause of Labour. James Connolly (cheers), oh, shades of Connolly, if you were only with us tonight to look with us upon the realisation of your great and many sacrifices (cheers).

However, these events in Waterford led to the misinterpretation of a Soviet Government coming into being in the city. The *Guardian* on 27 April reported that the city had been 'taken over by a Soviet Commissioner' while the same week the *Daily Herald* detailed stories of Waterford's 'Red Guards'.

The mayor of the city, Dr Vincent White, further blurred the lines when he congratulated the Soviet Government of Waterford and said that its opportunity to demonstrate its powers would not have to wait long. Though historian Emmett O'Connor concludes of the strike that 'if the soviet was political theatre, Waterford Workers' Council's ambition to demonstrate possibilities were real enough … events in Waterford were acquiring mythical proportions … Whether Waterford's action deserves to be called a soviet or not, that's what it meant.'

ROSAMOND JACOB:
Suffragette and Writer

Born on 13 October 1888, Rosamond Jacob was educated at the Newtown School from the age of 10. After one year, she reverted to home schooling. She joined the Gaelic League and was a founder member of the Waterford branch of Sinn Fein in 1906. An advocate for female suffrage, she opposed Redmondism on the basis of the lack of provision for the franchise of women, and as an Irish republican considered the First World War to be an imperial one. As the Waterford delegate to the Sinn Fein convention in 1917, Jacob obtained a pledge by the party to female franchise.

By 1920, she had moved to Dublin and became secretary of the Irishwomen's International League which she represented at congresses in Vienna (1921) and Prague (1929) for the Women's International League for Peace and Freedom. Initially she opposed the Anglo-Irish Treaty in 1921 but subsequently called for a cessation of hostilities in the civil war. She eventually left Sinn Fein in 1926 and joined Fianna Fail.

As a novelist, her first book, *Callaghan*, was published in 1920 under the pen name of 'F. Winthrop'. Seventeen years later, her study *The rise of the United Irishmen, 1791–1794* was well received and allowed her to obtain a publisher for her second novel, *The Troubled House* (originally written in 1921). She died in Dublin on 11 October 1960.

THE COLISEUM:
Waterford's First Cinema

The Coliseum was located at Adelphi Quay and was housed in a building which was built for a skating rink that closed in 1913. It was acquired by the Animated Picture Company which introduced moving pictures, or films, to Waterford. An orchestra was employed full-time. It was initially named the Rink Picture Palace and renamed the Coliseum in 1915. The first film shown under its new guise was *The Fatal Legacy* which starred Swedish actress Anna Q. Nilsson.

As Waterford's first cinema, it was run by Southern Coliseums Ltd, which later became Amusements Ltd. Frank O'Donoghue in his book *Goin' to the Pictures* described the Coliseum as having 'an unassuming appearance; no neoclassical lines or art deco façade; more like a large shed with a curved corrugated roof. The entrance was at the street corner, with the ticket box just inside and virtually no vestibule.' It was basic and managed by Miss Ellen Kerr from Carrick-on-Suir. She was nicknamed 'Olive Oyl' because of her resemblance to the cartoon character of Popeye's girlfriend.

Visiting the Col, as it was known locally, was a popular pastime in the 1940s and '50s, but with television becoming increasingly popular it closed in January 1966. It was bought by the Waterford Harbour Commissioners as a storage space. In 1984, it was made a store before falling into a state of disrepair. The building was finally demolished in 1992.

ST OTTERAN'S SCHOOL:
The First Montessori School in Ireland

The Italian educationalist Maria Montessori (and Italy's first female doctor), whose system of education bears her name, saw children as being 'serious-minded' and that they should develop at their own pace with encouragement and support from their teachers. By the 1920s, she developed a teacher training course in her methods in London, where Mrs Eleanora Gibbon of Rathcullaheen House, Ferrybank, and Sister Gertrude Allen of the Convent of the Mercy attended. Under the guidance of Mother de Sales Lowry, a Montessori programme was instigated, with the Junior Section of St Otteran's School in Philip Street in 1920 thus being the first Montessori school in Ireland. In the same year, these teaching practices could be found in a section of the Friends' School at Newtown. By 1925, another Montessori school had been established at the Ursuline Convent.

In June of the following year, the poet William Butler Yeats visited the Mercy in his capacity as a senator investigating the state of the Irish education system. Impressed by the creativity of the students who read poems they had composed, Yeats was inspired to write the poem 'Among School Children'. In 1927 Dr Maria Montessori visited Ireland for the first time, and the St Otteran's School on 27 June. She commented in the Visitors Book:

> I have been favourably impressed by what I have experienced here and I shall never forget it. Perfection in your work and vitality in your aspirations: this is, in brief, what I have admired in your establishment, where already I have a desire to return.

Montessori visited the school again ten years later with her son Mario. The notoriety of the school led to visits from figures from China and Holland. Sadly, in 1961, the Montessori school building at the Mercy was demolished, though Sister Gertrude Allen continued to be an advocate of the Montessori system at a new school on Military Road before retiring in 1970. Gradually, the school would revert to the Department of Education Curriculum for Primary Schools.

LIONEL RICHARDSON:
'the Greatest Daffodil Grower in the World'

I wandered lonely as a cloud
That floats on high o'er vales and hills,
When all at once I saw a crowd,

A host, of golden daffodils;
Beside the lake, beneath the trees,
Fluttering and dancing in the breeze.

William Wordsworth, 'I Wandered Lonely as A Cloud (Daffodils)'

Born in Tramore, County Waterford, Lionel Richardson lived at Weston before moving to Prospect House at Kilcohan in Waterford City. He was educated at Malvern College, and upon leaving Cambridge Union he frequently visited the Daffodil Gardens at Browdie Prestigne in Radnorshire and Guy Wilson of Antrim. The *Waterford News and Star* outlined that 'these visits inspired a great interest in daffodil growing and the development of highly specialised bulbs'. His 'breeding' of daffodils began with acquiring material from the gardens at Lisadell, sparing no expense in his endeavour to develop an impressive collection. A chance of a pollinated seed on 'Mary Copeland' opened the way for his many excellent double daffodils. Richardson's bulbs would be named after Irish towns such as Blarney and Kenmare, or renowned racecourses to battles such as Matapan and Narvik. As an amateur, he exhibited his daffodils at flower shows in London after the end of the First World War. Richardson displayed his flowers for the first time at the Royal Horticultural Society Show in Dublin in 1915, winning the Lord Ardilaun Cup for a collection of fifty varieties.

From 1922, he relinquished his amateur status (the pursuit becoming too expensive to just be a hobby); his passion for cultivating daffodils became a successful business, with the United States a popular destination for his bulbs. Exhibiting at shows in Birmingham, London and America allowed him to demonstrate his skill in horticulture. By 1927, he had won numerous gold medals at gardening exhibitions in Dublin and London as well as garnering five first prizes for his daffodils at the Horticultural Hall in London that year. The previous year his engagement to Miss Helen Clibborn of Silverspring, Clonmel, County Tipperary, was announced; she would also go on to win the Peter Barr Memorial Cup in 1960 for daffodil growing, an honour which her husband was bestowed in 1931 by the Royal Horticultural Society.

Lionel Richardson would go on to win the Engleheart Cup twenty-two times, the Midland Daffodil Society's Bourne, Cartwright and Leamington

Cups on numerous occasions as well as sixty-four gold medals and copious numbers of first-class certificates for his cultivation of daffodils. The Engleheart Cup, named in honour of Rev. George Engleheart for his revolutionary endeavours in cultivating daffodils, was established in 1913 by the Royal Horticultural Society. It is awarded annually to the display of the best twelve daffodils of all bred and raised from seed by the exhibitor. It is the most coveted award at the RHS's Daffodil Show in London.

The business side of Richardson's passion is illustrated in the *Irish Independent* from May 1940:

> Some of his bulbs command quite fantastic prices. These bulbs can be obtained through Messrs. Sir James W. Mackey, Ltd., 23 Upper O'Connell St., Dublin, while Messrs. Knowles and Son, the well-known Grafton St. florists, are acting as agents for sale of the blooms. They are making special window displays of these which are attracting admiring crowds.

A variety of daffodil he cultivated named 'Krakatoa', named after the volcanic island between Java and Sumatra, could fetch up to £100 for a single bulb. The Dutch journalist Kees Van Hoek noted that Richardson 'would only sell the four he had of that variety for a cool thousand. Hence, of his more exclusive varieties, five pounds a bulb is about the moderate average price!' At the Royal Horticultural Society show in London in 1945 Richardson's 'Krakatoa' was 'the most admired of a conspicuous feature'. It had taken Richardson fifteen years to acquire the quality of bulbs to then develop them to perfection.

In 1941, he was awarded the Gold Medal of Honour by the Royal Horticultural Society of Ireland for his 'conspicuous service to horticulture'. The *Munster Express* opined in 1942 that 'he [Richardson] even sent blooms to Holland, which is something like exporting tea from Ireland to China' such was the quality and reputation he had developed in the horticulture world. He was even invited to judge at the Heemsteed Annual Show in the Netherlands.

His gardens were visited by van Hoek in 1945, who wrote that:

> We went through the gardens where, in 175 beds, spread more like so many low mattresses on the earth, each carefully covered by sea sand like a porous eiderdown, the daffodils had already begun pushing up their green stalks.

In a good month's time these huge wards of beds (each bed sixty-five feet long by three feet wide) will have their protective screens around them, made of Kentish hop and six feet high, preventing the wind from spoiling the blooms. I have seldom seen outside Holland such spotless order, such perfect regimentation, as if pensioned sergeant-majors had been recruited as gardeners, for even the stalks grew as if along invisible ruler. In a special treasure plot neat slates divide the bulbous growths. No wonder that even the Dutch have felt that here was a man from whom they could learn, and invited him to judge at their world-famous floral Shows.

In his fiftieth year of raising daffodils, Richardson became only the second Irishman after Sir Frederick Moore to be made a vice president of the Royal Horticultural Society. Over the course of his thirty-six years of competing at the Royal Horticultural Society's shows, he also won the P.D. Williams medal several times and the Veitch Memorial gold medal for his services in the cultivation of daffodils. The *Irish Times* stated that he 'won widespread fame in 1958 by developing a pink-cupped daffodil – the first with a colour other than yellow'.

Upon his death on 17 October 1961 an appreciation in the *Irish Times* by a W.J.T. finished with:

Those who knew him best will miss him most, for he was the perfect embodiment of a gentleman, shy, unassuming and of unswerving integrity. He was kind and generous to a fault, while his judgement was level-headed and wise at all times.

There is a rich symbolism in the fact that the flowers he created will come to life at the time when we commemorate the Resurrection of our Lord. Here, indeed, is comfort for those who are bereaved. This is His gracious message to the mourner, the proof and pledge of life eternal.

A reflection of the times in which Lionel Richardson lived, the idea of Richardson's work coming to life every spring would appear to be a most fitting thought.

Helen Richardson would continue to grow daffodils after the death of her husband, going on to win twenty gold medals at the Royal Horticultural Society show. She was the subject of a John McCarten article for the *New*

Yorker magazine in 1971 detailing the maintenance of her husband's work and legacy as well as her own career as a horticulturalist. Nearly thirty years after van Hoek's visit, McCarten stated:

> There are about 100,000 bulbs planted in the fields around Prospect House. There are roughly 350 named varieties, but hundreds more never develop into anything worth cultivating or christening. It takes 5 years to transform a daffodil seed into a bulb, and out of 5,000 seeds you'd be lucky to be rewarded with 200 bulbs you wanted to keep. Prospect House has 80 customers in the U.S. Pedigrees are so important that she has them detailed on a computer-it's known as George-which is used by Dr. Tom Throckmorton, who lives in Des Moines, Iowa. Head gardener, Jack Goldsmith has been there 43 years. They sent 170 blooms to the London show recently – 190 varieties – but usually they send more. The flowers are endlessly varied in color, not just the familiar yellow. Prospect House isn't devoted exclusively to daffodils. Mrs. R. grows tomato plants for the market and has a fine big herd of Jersey cattle. She also has an old-fashioned Victorian garden.

She continued to develop daffodils and kept track of them with the most advance of technology. The admiration of Richardson bulbs still exists, with the American Daffodil Society noting of the legacy of the Richardsons that their 'flowers were known for the depth of color in the red/orange cups of the flowers'.

A remarkable man who found a kindred spirit in Helen Clibborn, it is interesting to think that from Kilcohan came one of the most renowned and innovative of horticulturalists, the subject of numerous newspaper articles, revered across the world with honours aplenty, and that the wonderful colours of their daffodils can still be seen with each spring.

> *For oft, when on my couch I lie*
> *In vacant or in pensive mood,*
> *They flash upon that inward eye*
> *Which is the bliss of solitude;*
> *And then my heart with pleasure fills,*
> *And dances with the daffodils.*

Aerial view of Waterford City, c. 1936. UK2873, Waterford County Museum

WATERFORD MUNICIPAL ART COLLECTION

'one of the hidden gems of the Irish art world'

Peter Jordan, Waterford Municipal Art Collection: A History and Catalogue (2006)

The origins of the Waterford Municipal Art Collection can be traced to the movement of developing a distinct cultural identity post the creation of the Irish Free State. Such a belief is demonstrated in a letter published in the *Waterford News* in 1935 which stated that the city had 'an important part to play in the reconstruction of the nation's cultural life' with the creation of a civic art collection being a way to explore that cultural identity.

In 1935, Arnold Marsh, head of Newtown School, and his wife Hilda Roberts, a painter, began staging exhibitions (the first of which was colour reproductions of works of the Old Masters) which would act as a preamble to the formation of a municipal art gallery. This would lead to artists such as Paul Henry, Mainie Jellet and Jack B. Yeats exhibiting their works in the city.

The housing of the collection was the endeavour of Edward J. Maguire. It was first based at the public library, then moving to 5 O'Connell Street in 1953. It wasn't until the 1980s that Finola O'Doherty, administrator at Garter Lane Arts Centre, began the process of cataloguing the collection.

Irish Times journalist Aidan Dunne noted in 2008 that:

> from Willem van der Hagen's 1736 view of Waterford to Donald Teskey's tempestuous urban landscape from 1994, it is now a lively and eclectic collection with some great surprises. These include fine works by Arthur Armstrong and George Campbell, a terrific Patrick Collins figure painting, one of Louis le Brocquy's representational compositions from 1941, several works donated by Dermod O'Brien, a good Annunciation by Patrick Pye and a textural abstract from 1958 by Camille Souter. This is not to mention pieces by Jack B Yeats, Herry Kernoff, Charles Lamb and William Leech. Patric Stevenson's topographical watercolours of Waterford are also outstanding.

The collection was based at Greyfriars, with works displayed at the Theatre Royal and Waterford University Hospital. Future developments will seek to have the art collection based in O'Connell Street as part of the creation of a cultural quarter of the city.

WATERFORD FC, 1930

Blue is the colour, football is the game,
We're all together, and winning is our aim,
So cheer us on through the wind and rain,
'cause Waterford, Waterford is our name.

The first incarnation of Waterford Football Club was when the club joined the League of Ireland in 1930. A brief absence from the league between 1932 to 1934 saw the Blues re-enter the competition for the 1934/35 season. Success followed in 1937, winning both the FAI Cup and the League of Ireland Shield.

From Here to Modernity: Twentieth-Century Waterford

In 1941, Waterford were on the cusp of winning a league and cup double but were pipped by Cork United in both competitions. Both sides had finished on level points in the league with a play-off needed to decide the winner. However, in a dispute between the players and the board of the club over payments, the club were unable to fulfil the fixture and the title was awarded to Cork United. The club resigned from the league following the incident but were reinstated for the 1945/46 campaign.

The golden age of Waterford soccer took place in the late 1960s and early 1970s, winning six League of Ireland titles in eight seasons. League success gained the club entry to the European Cup and they played ties against Manchester United and Glasgow Celtic. The late Waterford poet and journalist with the *Cork Examiner,* Sean Dunne, wrote in his 1991 autobiography *In My Father's House*: 'After leaving primary school in John's Park ... The Waterford soccer team was winning game after game. As they won, their support grew and the games in Kilcohan Park were drawing huge crowds ... Soccer was a foreign sport.'

A foreword by Jimmy Magee to Brian Kennedy's history of the club, *Singing the Blues*, notes:

> From the autumn of 1965 to the spring of 1973 Waterford gave Irish football a galaxy of stars. A few names to jog the memory – Alfie Hale one of Ireland's best ever, Jimmy McGeough a brilliant wing half (midfielder in modern jargon), Peter Fitzgerald of a famous clan, Shamie Coad the 'major', Vinny Maguire, Tommy Taylor, John O'Neill, Al Casey, Peter Bryan and two mighty imports from Coventry, Peter Thomas and Johnny Matthews.

Names to still the childish play of many a youngster, the group delivered six league titles. They entered the Royal Showband, shimming like snakes, and the great entertainers of Kilcohan scored goals galore. The return of Paddy Coad as manager was the return of the prodigal son. Mick Lynch led the charge, scoring seventeen goals as Waterford won their first league title in the same year England claimed its only World Cup at Wembley in 1966. In the consciousness of those Suirside, Johnny Matthews would rival any of Alf Ramsey's side with his elegance. He arrived in Waterford on St Patrick's Day (jokingly believing the parade was a celebration of his signing) for what he believed was a six-week loan deal. Thirteen years later he finally left Waterford for Limerick.

In 1980, Waterford won the FAI Cup for the second time, with Brian Gardner scoring the winning goal against St Patrick's Athletic. Two years later the club changed its name to Waterford United. The introduction of a two division/tier League of Ireland in 1985/86 saw the club reach the FAI Cup Final again in 1986 but lose to Shamrock Rovers 2–0.

The Blues were relegated to the First Division in 1988/89. The rest of the twentieth century saw the club yo-yo from the Premier to the First Division, with Waterford United suffering relegations in 1991, 1993 and 2000. The club achieved promotion to the top division in 1992 (finishing as runners-up to Limerick in the First Division), 1998 (by winning the First Division) and in 2002/03 under the managerial reign of former player Jimmy McGeough.

The League of Ireland changed to a summer league for the 2003 campaign, with Waterford finishing the season in sixth place. The 2004 season saw former Republic of Ireland international Paul McGrath appointed Director of Football and Alan Reynolds as player-manager. The club finished fifth and reached its first FAI Cup Final since 1986.

Waterford's wait for FAI Cup success continues. The club had some difficult seasons after being relegated from the Premier Division in 2007 and finally gained promotion back to the top flight in 2017. The same year, the club reverted to the name Waterford FC.

Some notable players to have played for the Blues and received international honours for the Republic of Ireland include: Con Martin, Shay Brennan, Alfie Hale, Al Finucane, Tommy McConville, Noel Hunt, Daryl Murphy and Sean Maguire. Other players to have played for the club include Bobby Tambling and Bobby Charlton (England internationals), Piotr Suski (Poland) and Ed McIllvenny (Scottish-born USA international) to name a few.

THE BLUESHIRTS IN WATERFORD CITY

On 23 May 1932, a meeting of the Army Comrades Association was held in Waterford City, chaired by Dr Vincent White, a former Sinn Fein Mayor and Cumann na nGaedheal TD. In total, 250 members joined that Waterford branch of the ACA that night. The group aimed to maintain respect for the state, commemorate the dead of the War of Independence as well as oppose Communism and defend the right of free speech. A number of fights occurred between Fianna Fail supporters and members of the ACA, who acted as guards at Cumann na nGaeheal public meetings.

February 1933 saw the ACA adopt a 'blue shirt' as a form of uniform, as well as Eoin O'Duffy being elected leader of the group. The group was renamed the National Guard. A meeting in the City Hall of Waterford City for that August was abandoned and efforts to stage the event at the Imperial Hotel were hampered by an outbreak of fighting. Yet that night, O'Duffy was approached to become the leader of an amalgamation of the ailing Cumann na nGaedheal and Centre Party (who represented the interests of farmers). This new party named Fine Gael saw O'Duffy visit the city two more times in November of that year, first a dance in the Large Room of City Hall and subsequently a speech at Ballybricken.

Violence erupted between April and July 1934 in the city. On Saturday, 28 April, members of Fine Gael were attacked outside their headquarters at Lady Lane before more of their supporters arrived to defend them. Normal order did not return until midnight and a small scuffle broke out again the following day.

Eugene Broderick notes 'the Blueshirts may have been stronger in Waterford City than in other places, due to the old Redmondite tradition and the association of Mrs Redmond with the organisation'. The Blueshirts adopted the symbols and traits of the proponents of fascism. Opposition would come from labour and trade union movements in the city, with a large demonstration held on the Mall on 31 May 1934 to condemn fascism. Yet the animosity between Fianna Fail and Fine Gael is a consequence of the Irish Civil War more than necessarily political ideology.

TERESA DEEVY:
Playwright

Teresa Deevy was born on 21 January 1894 at Landscape, Passage Road, in Waterford. Her maternal grandfather, John Feehan, had been a mayor of the city. The youngest of thirteen, Deevy was encouraged by her mother to write short stories of everyday events that occurred in the house. She went to school at the Ursuline before starting a Bachelor of Arts at University College Dublin in 1913. However, she contracted Meniere's disease which led her to transfer to University College Cork where she could attend the Cork Eye, Ear and Throat Hospital. Unfortunately, she was unable to complete her studies due to her growing deafness and went to London in 1914 to learn lipreading.

While in London, she read the plays of Anton Chekov, Henrik Ibsen and George Bernard Shaw and would then watch them performed in theatres. In 1919, she returned to her birthplace, where she joined Cumann na mBan and would visit Republican prisoners at the jail in Ballybricken. Deevy had a number of articles published in the national press and in 1925 she submitted her plays to the Abbey Theatre for consideration. Eventually, her play *Reapers* was staged at the Abbey in 1930.

A twelve-year association with the Abbey saw plays such as *The King of Spain's Daughter, Katie Roche* and *The Wild Goose* all staged in 1936. She also adapted many of her plays for radio, in addition to new works specifically for the medium, aired up to 1958. *The King of Spain's Daughter* and *In Search of Valour* were adapted to television and broadcast by the BBC.

One of her most critically acclaimed plays was the *Wife of James Whelan*; rejected by the Abbey in 1942, it was staged at the Studio Theatre Club in Dublin in 1956. The following year a play on the life of Luke Wadding was aired on Radio Eireann. She returned to her birthplace in the latter years of her life and died on 19 January 1963.

SEEING THE WORLD ON WHEELS:
Dervla Murphy Educated at the Ursuline

The travel writer Dervla Murphy, born in Lismore, County Waterford in 1931, was educated at the Ursuline Convent in Waterford City. In 1965, her first book and bestseller titled *Full Tilt* detailed her journey from Ireland to India on a bicycle. A hallmark of her writing is her humour and inquisitiveness, which has seen her write about her travels in Northern Ireland, Central and South Africa, as well as the Balkans.

WATERFORD CORPORATION DISSOLVED, 4 MAY 1937

On 4 May 1937, Sean T. O'Kelly, Minister for Local Government and Public Health, issued an order to dissolve Waterford Corporation after the result of an inquiry held in September and October 1936. Mr P.J. Megan was appointed commissioner with the duties of the council now encompassed in his position. The first meeting of the new commissioner was 14 October 1937 in City Hall, though there was some confusion when the city's mayor, James Aylward, refused to agree to the dissolution order, and there was also a suspension of Waterford's highest civic office. Under the Waterford City Managers Act 1939, a City Council was established with a body of fifteen councillors who would be elected by the public. The first meeting of this body took place in November 1939.

WATERFORD MEN AND THE SPANISH CIVIL WAR

The conflict between the democratically elected Republican government and Nationalists led by General Franco spilt Irish opinion. The Catholic Church, the majority of the media and considerable public opinion supported the Nationalists, particularly when there were reports of alleged violence towards members of the clergy by Republican forces. The Irish government under the leadership of Eamon de Valera took a neutral stance towards the war in Spain.

Eoin O'Duffy, the leader of the quasi-fascist Blueshirts, raised an Irish Brigade to aid the fight of General Franco's forces but it would see little combat. These 700 Irishmen were known as the 'Angels of Monasterevin' and formed part of the XV Bandera Irlandesa del Terico of the Spanish Foreign Legion, returning to Ireland in 1937.

Frank Ryan led the Connolly Column of the International Brigade which numbered between 150 to 200 Irish Republicans to support the Spanish Republican government. They were involved in combat and sustained many casualties.

There is a memorial to eleven Waterford men who fought with the 15th International Brigade in Spain which is located next to the Bishop's Palace.

They were Frank Edwards, Jackie Hunt, John Kelly, Harry Kennedy, Jackie Lennon, Peter O'Connor, John O'Shea, the Power brothers (Johnny, Paddy and Willie) and Mossie Quinlan who died at the Jarama Front.

One of the combatants, Frank Edwards, was dismissed from his position as a teacher in Mount Sion on the directive of Bishop Kinnane for not renouncing his membership of the Republican Congress.

The monument is made from an 8-tonne block of Spanish granite which was sculpted by Michael Warren of Wexford, with Waterford City Council becoming the first local authority in the Republic of Ireland to commemorate members of the International Brigade in 2004.

JOHN J. HEARNE:
The Architect of *Bunreacht na hEireann* 1937

John Joseph Hearne was central to the drafting of the Irish Constitution, *Bunreacht na hEireann*, with some commentators stating that he was the architect of the document. Born in Waterford, he was the son of Richard Hearne who was one of Ireland's first boot manufacturers and also served as mayor of the city (in 1901 and 1903). He was educated at Waterpark in the city before obtaining a BA and LLB from the National University of Ireland in Dublin. Hearne had studied for a time at St Patrick's College, Maynooth, to become a priest but pursued a career in law by studying for the bar at King's Inn, and called to the bar in 1919. Upon the outbreak of the Irish Civil War, Hearne joined the Free State army, reaching the rank of commandant. He resigned from the army in November 1923.

He worked as an assistant parliamentary draughtsman from 1923 to 1929. Undoubtedly, his experience in this position aided his role in the drafting of the Irish constitution in 1937. Hearne became a legal advisor to the Department of External Affairs from 1929 to 1939. The leader of Fianna Fáil, Eamon de Valera recognised Hearne's ability and gave him the responsibility for drafting the bill which abolished the oath of allegiance. After the constitution came into effect on 29 December 1939, de Valera gifted a copy of the document to Hearne writing, 'Architect-in-Chief and Draftsman … in testimony of the fundamental part he took in framing this, the Free Constitution of the Irish People'.

In 1939, Hearne was appointed the first High Commissioner to Canada, which he served until 1949. From 1950 to 1960 he was Irish Ambassador to the United States of America and began the tradition of presenting a bowl of shamrocks to the President at the White House on St Patrick's Day.

MARLOWE'S WATERFORD CONNECTION:
Raymond Chandler

The American noir-fiction writer Raymond Chandler was the son of Florence Thornton who hailed from Waterford City. Chandler wrote that his mother was 'of a Quaker family' (though no such records exist to prove this) and that many of his 'Irish relatives, some poor, some not poor, and all Protestant, and some of them Sinn Féiners and some of them entirely pro-British'.

Chandler's father was an alcoholic and his behaviour led to Florence fleeing to Ireland and subsequently London. The Chicago-born writer attended Dulwich College (the same college as P.G. Wodehouse) which was paid for by his uncle Ernest Thornton. During his teenage years, Chandler still visited his mother's hometown, and is recalled by local writer Bill Long perusing Power's second-hand bookshop.

After completing his studies at Dulwich, Chandler took exams for the civil service in England before sailing to the United States. In 1917, he joined the Canadian army to fight in France. After the war, he took a correspondence course in bookkeeping and worked in the oil industry.

His debut novel, *The Big Sleep*, introduced the character of Californian private detective Philip Marlowe, later

Lauren Bacall and Humphrey Bogart watching from the sidelines as *The Big Sleep* was being filmed, December 1946.

played by Hollywood legend Humphrey Bogart. The book is considered an American classic.

In a conversation with Bill Long he outlined a Marlowe novel to be set in Waterford City. John Flynn and Jerry Kelleher's *Waterford Journeys in America* details:

> Marlowe is visiting Ireland and he stops off in Waterford for a few days. He visits a bar on the quays and there witnesses a fight between sailors from different ships. The next day he hears that one of the sailors from the fight has been murdered and that the body has been found in Stickyback's (the nickname for Power's second-hand bookshop) doorway. That evening Marlowe is recognised by the captain of the murdered sailor's vessel and is asked to investigate.

UNEMPLOYED MEN'S CLUB, WATERFORD, 1940–45

From the establishment of the Irish Free State in 1922, unemployment steadily increased in the city. The active labour force fell from 8,017 in 1926 to 7,625 ten years later. Just over 90 per cent of single women were unemployed in Waterford in 1936, while the figure for single men stood at nearly 53 per cent.

A meeting in the People's Park in October 1932 saw Thomas Purdue state:

> We should see that we are treated as human beings. It is now or never, and our grievances should no longer be left in abeyance. If unemployment is not dealt with as a national question, it will become a living cancer on the life of the state. We exceed in number, by far, any other party in the country, and our demands are the largest. It is up to you to concentrate on the goal you set before yourselves … work for every unemployed man.

An Unemployed Men's Club was established in the city and operated at Airmount House in 1940. The *Irish Press* considered the venture to be the first 'provincial' Mount Street Club. For five years it allowed men to exchange services for goods but would gradually decline due to emigration.

RAF PLANE CRASH, 17 FEBRUARY 1943

A British Wellington bomber crash-landed in a field by Six Cross Roads at Kilbarry near Waterford City. The aircraft carried a crew of five and was returning from a bombing raid in Lorient on U-boat pens. The instruments of the plane failed, leading it to split from its squadron. It circled over Waterford City, eventually running out of fuel and landing in the field. The crew were uninjured and subsequently interned in the Curragh (after receiving much attention from Waterford locals who took pieces of the Wellington bomber as a souvenir) and returned to Britain in June 1944.

BALLYBRICKEN JAIL WALL DISASTER, MARCH 1943

The deaths of nine people and injuries to seventeen others (one of whom would die weeks later, bringing the number of fatalities to ten) happened as a result of the collapse of the jail wall of Ballybricken, which was the worst peacetime tragedy in the city. The disused jail was inhabited by the army during the years of the Emergency, with turf being stored there. It appears that this combined with damp conditions led to the 60ft wall collapsing around 12:45 on the morning of 4 March, which demolished four houses and caused extensive damage to three others at King's Terrace.

The youngest victim was 2-year-old Betty Stewart. The following Friday saw the funerals of the victims take place. The hearses went from St Patrick's Hospital to the cathedral with a military guard provided by the Army No. 3 Band. An inquest found that the collapse of the wall was due to too much turf being stacked against the wall and the damp conditions leading to the turf becoming heavy. Forty years after the tragic events a plaque was erected at Jail Street.

In 2006 a memorial was unveiled on Ballybricken Green to commemorate the victims of the disaster.

WATERFORD GLASS:
From a Local Glass Factory to a Global Crystal Brand

A hand-blown lead crystal was developed by the Quaker brothers George and William Penrose in 1783. It won several gold medals at the great London Exhibition in 1851. However, this factory closed in 1851. The glass industry in the city was revitalised by a Czechoslovakian glass manufacturer named Charles Bačik who moved to Waterford after his business, which specialised in hand-cut glass, was taken over by Communist authorities. Bačik and his family moved to the city in 1946 and with the support of investors such as the Waterford Corporation and Dubliner jeweller Bernard Fitzpatrick opened a factory in Ballytruckle in April 1947.

The first employee of the new factory was Miroslav Havel, a compatriot of Bačik, hired for a three-month stint which extended to his residing in Waterford for the rest of his life. The pair trained local workers, saw a glass technology course introduced at the Central Technical Institute on Parnell Street and recruited craftsmen from Germany to aid the fledgling factory. Initially, it focused on cutting and engraving imported Belgian soda glass (which was free of import duty tax). Havel studied glass pieces from the original Penrose factory in the National Museum, producing full-scale drawings which would inspire the future collections of Waterford Crystal. The addition of German salesman Franz Marckwald was to increase sales as the business sought to move from low-end soda glass for the Irish market to a global brand specialising in premium pieces of crystal.

The brand was enhanced in 1950 by former Cumann na nGaedheal minister Joseph McGrath when he assumed control of the company, his wealth stemming from the Irish Hospitals' Sweepstakes. The appointment of Joseph and Noel Griffin as managing director and general manager, respectively, led to a focus on increasing the technology used in production. A new plant was built at Johnstown near to the old gasworks. Production started in 1951 with a staff of 300 and saw the first crystal glass produced in the city for over 100 years.

Its most popular pattern was the Lismore range (launched in 1952) created by Miroslav Havel who became the chief designer at the factory. As Tom Hunt notes, the 'diamond-shaped wedge cuts that referenced the original Penrose crystal distinguished these pieces and became Waterford Crystal's most identifiable characteristic'. Further foreign influence on the craftsmanship can be seen with the appointment of the Romanian Joseph Cretzan to train apprentice blowers, and Kurt Berger, a German who was an expert in mould making.

The company made a profit for the first time in 1955 and would form Waterford Glass Incorporated to transact directly with stores in the United States. The 'Collect Waterford' marketing campaign, combined with the ability to collect numerous suites of Waterford Crystal in high-end stores, made it a huge success in the States. In 1966, Waterford Glass became a public company. The following year, 1967, saw Jacqueline Kennedy tour the factory and order Waterford glass chandeliers in 1971 for the Kennedy Centre in Washington. Sean McMahon and Jo O'Donoghue believed this 'association cemented the product's popularity among Irish-Americans'.

Special commissions such as these chandeliers, or a scale replica of the Statue of Liberty gifted by Taoiseach Garrett Fitzgerald to American President Ronald Reagan in 1986, continued to demonstrate the quality of the product and increase the visibility of the brand. This would also be seen in Waterford Crystal creating trophies for various sports events from tennis to golf.

In 1973, a new factory was built at Kilbarry encompassing 450,000 square feet with additional factories established in Dungarvan (1970) and Butlerstown specialising in lighting (in 1979). This would prove to be the zenith of the company's powers. The year 1990 saw huge losses, redundancies and strikes take place, leading to a Sir Anthony O'Reilly consortium investing in the company. New cost-cutting measures led to outsourcing of the product, while the introduction of a John Rocha range of glassware proved popular. The crafting of a crystal ball for the Times Square, New Year's Eve Millennium ceremony brought renewed attention to the company with the event being viewed by 1.2 billion people. However, this was a temporary upturn rather than the beginning of long-term success. The Dungarvan plant closed in 2005 followed by the plant at Kilbarry in 2009.

The fallout saw staff stage unofficial sit-ins to retain jobs which didn't succeed. A drawn-out legal battle ensued over workers' pensions which was not resolved until 2015. A new holding company was created and acquired by Fiskars Corporation in 2015, which run the House of Waterford Crystal now located on the Mall.

EDWARD WALSH:
Ireland's Oldest Coachman

Edward Walsh died aged 95 at 16 Green Street, Waterford City in 1951. Some of the notable passengers that Walsh drove included Charles Stewart Parnell when he was made a freeman of the city in the nineteenth century to Sir James Power when he was knighted by King Edward VII in 1904. He worked for Cummins Posting (the location of the present Granville Hotel) and Morrissey undertakers at Parnell Street. Walsh assisted in the funerals of four bishops and in 1931 was present at the funeral of a fifth, Bishop Hackett. Later years saw Walsh drive a horse bus for the Granville Hotel and subsequently the Imperial Hotel.

ANNIE BROPHY:
Waterford's First Female Photographer

Born at Johnstown in Waterford, Annie Brophy worked as a photographer from 1922 to 1978. She trained at Hughes Photographers in Manor Street before setting up her own operation at 9 Barker Street. She was the first female photographer in the city and one of the first in Ireland. Brophy photographed the aftermath of the Ballybricken Jail Wall disaster in 1943. Her 60,000 negatives and prints were bought by Waterford City Council and are stored by Waterford City and County Archives.

'AGAINST THE TIDE':
Noel Browne, Minister for Health, 1948–51

Born in Waterford in 1915, Noel Browne studied at Trinity College, Dublin, and qualified as a doctor. Over the course of his childhood he lived in Derry and Athlone due to his father's work as an inspector for the National Society for the Prevention of Cruelty to Children. Upon the death of his father when Browne was 9 years old the family moved to his mother's home place of Ballinrobe. After contracting tuberculosis, he became an activist for the eradication of the disease which had taken the lives of both his parents. Browne's mother died after she moved the family to England. TB would also kill two of his siblings.

In England he achieved a scholarship to Beaumont College, a Jesuit School, and his medical studies were financed by his friend's family, their surname being Chance. The patriarch of the family was Arthur Chance, a surgeon, who also paid for Browne's medical treatment when he suffered a resurgence of TB during his studies in 1940. He recovered at Midhurst in Sussex and completed his studies in 1942. Browne became a medical intern at Dr Stevens' Hospital in Dublin and worked in a number of sanatoria in England and Ireland. Yet it was his belief that it was only through politics that he could meaningfully combat the disease which had ravaged his family.

He was elected to the Dáil as a member of the Clann na Poblachta party, which formed part of the first Inter-party government. On his first day in parliament, Browne was made Minister for Health aged 33 years of age. His crusade against TB resulted in the near extinction of the disease in the Republic of Ireland. His use of the hospital sweepstakes funding aided the development of a system of sanatoria to make the most of the introduction of the BCG vaccine. Browne also established the first Irish national blood transfusion service.

Browne's efforts to introduce the Mother and Child Scheme resulted in opposition for the hierarchy of the Catholic Church and later the fall of the government in 1951. The bill was to implement free health care for all children under 16 years of age and the same provision for all mothers. Opposition to the bill arose from the belief that it would lead to liberal family planning and the introduction of contraception. However, the incident that caused the fall of the government was when rural independents withdrew their support due to the failure to raise the price of milk.

He continued to hold his seat in Dublin as an independent member but ran for Fianna Fáil in the 1954 election, losing his seat. The intervening years would see him stand as a candidate in numerous elections for parties such as the National Progressive Democratic Party (of which he was a co-founder), the Labour Party and the Socialist Labour Party. Browne retired from politics in February 1982. The historian John A. Murphy believed that this nomadic political existence was to 'restore his dream of creating a socially just Ireland'.

He spent the majority of his later life in Connemara, and his autobiography *Against the Tide* published in 1986 was a bestseller. Browne was mooted to run for the presidency in 1990 but this was rejected by Dick Spring, leader of the Labour Party, who was an advocate for Mary Robinson. She became the seventh President of Ireland and the first female to hold the office.

Browne died in Galway on 22 May 1997.

AMBASSADOR OF STYLE:
Sybil Connolly, Fashion Designer

Sybil Connolly was a fashion designer whose 'hand-crafted' style designs were worn by Jackie Kennedy and Elizabeth Taylor. Connolly was born in Swansea to a Welsh mother, her father being from Waterford. Upon the death of her father, who was an insurance salesman, Connolly and her mother moved to Waterford, with her being educated at the Convent of Mercy school. Her natural talent for fashion led her to move to London aged 17. She returned to Ireland around 1939.

Connolly's trademark was pleated linen and she kept prices lower than her European competitors. The material allowed for it to be packed away without creases, which proved popular with women of the day.

Connolly never married but, when asked about the issue, commented to the *Daily Mail* in 1957 that 'for the moment, I like to buy my mink and diamonds myself'. The same year, she moved to 71 Merrion Square which became her own workrooms, which she referred to as 'the house that linen built'.

Her ability to publicise her product was also part of her success, with Eleanor Lambert referring to her as an ambassador for Ireland in the promotion of her work and country coming in equal measure.

Towards the end of her career she turned to interior design, such as the refurbishment of the Swiss Cottage in County Tipperary and designing tableware for Tiffany and Co. She died in Dublin on 7 May 1998.

PADDY COAD:
Mister League of Ireland

Paddy Coad, often regarded as the best player who didn't transfer to an English club from the League of Ireland, was undoubtedly one of the most well-known and revered names in Irish soccer. Comfortable and confident on the left side, whether it was in the defence or attack, he gained eleven caps for his country. One of his finest moments for his country was his substitute appearance against Norway in Oslo in 1951, scoring the winning goal in a 3–2 victory.

Born in Waterford, Coad made his debut for his local side at the age of 17 in 1937, though he would later be transferred to Northern Irish side Glenavon due to Waterford FC's financial difficulties the following season. The outbreak of the Second World War led Coad to return to his hometown club in 1939. He came to prominence in the 1940/41 season as inside forward for Waterford FC which was beaten by Cork United in the Free State Cup final after a replay.

That season would also be noted for the fact that Waterford would finish level with their cup final opponents as top of the league, but would later resign from the league due to a dispute between the players and the directors of the club over the non-payment of bonuses, leading to the Cork United winning the league due to the Blues' failure to fulfil the playoff fixture. Moving to Shamrock Rovers as the result of Waterford going out of business, he would go on to win three League of Ireland titles and four FAI Cups with the Milltown club. From 1943 to 1955, Coad and Jimmy Dunne were Rovers' only two full-time professionals.

Becoming player-coach of the Hoops in 1949 after the sudden death of Jimmy Dunne (former Sheffield United and Arsenal forward) saw the creation of 'Coad's Colts' who the *Irish Independent* noted brought 'a glamour and excitement to the local game'. In addition, he would attend coaching courses in England, which was a departure in the League of Ireland at the time. His 'Colts' were a side made up of young talented players such as Liam Tuohy and Ronnie Nolan. In fact, Coad basically acquired the whole international schoolboy's team to create a side that focused on keeping possession and progressing up the field with pace.

Waterford City across the River Suir, *c.* 1960. *UK1270, Waterford County Museum*

Under his guidance, Rovers would achieve two league crowns and two FAI Cup victories. However, the most noteworthy chapter in Coad's coaching career was that of his side's performance against the 'Busby Babes' of Manchester United in the European Cup in 1957 (the season of the tragic Munich Air disaster). Many would observe that Rovers were more than a match for their English opponents for skill but were unable to overcome the gap in fitness levels.

The fairy tale that one could term Coad's career would finish 'happily ever after' when he returned to Waterford in 1960 as player/manager and led that club to its first league victory in 1966. In total, Paddy Coad scored 126 League of Ireland goals over a twenty-five-year playing career.

TEDDY BOYS AND MODS

The 1950s saw 'Teddy Boy' culture, as showcased in the film *Blackboard Jungle* in 1956, arrive in Ireland. The film itself was shown at the Coliseum cinema at Adelphi Quay between 1956 and 1958. It amalgamated Edwardian dress sense with listening to American rock n' roll, a combination that struck fear in the hearts of older generations. Though in England there was violence associated with 'Teddy Boys', this was less so in Ireland. One Waterford boy would receive a two-month jail sentence for being part of a gang that broke into a number of premises in the city and intimidated pedestrians.

The 1960s would see the 'Teddy Boys' give way to the 'Mods', with a brief period when skinheads overtook them, the 'Mods' becoming popular again in the 1980s. This led to increased tension in the local media that warned of an invasion of young men on scooters that would culminate in violence to rival that of the Battle of Brighton Beach. However, this did not occur, and like all fads it passed.

THE GREEN MAN:
Waterford City's First Set of Traffic Lights

Waterford City's first set of traffic lights were placed at the junction of Parnell Street and John Street and came into use in January 1962. Previously, a member of the Garda Siochana was on duty directing traffic from the location. Costing £2,000, they functioned by detector pads on the road.

WATERFORD CITY AND POPULAR MUSIC IN THE TWENTIETH CENTURY

THE ROYAL: MUSIC HALLS AND DANCE CRAZES

A feature of Irish social life for the youth of the 1960s was to go to dance halls where music was performed by showbands that played covers of popular music of the day. These groups began to appear in 1956–57 and were well established by 1960–61, with one of the most renowned being the Royal Showband from Waterford City, whose lead singer was Brendan Bowyer.

Beginning their music journey performing at the Olympia and Arundel ballrooms, the Royal went on to top the Irish charts and became the only Irish band to win the Carl Alen Award in England for outstanding dance band.

Their success saw them reach Las Vegas. The band numbered Jim Conlon on guitar, Michael Coppinger on sax, Jerry Cullen on piano, Charlie Matthews as drummer, Eddie Sullivan on trumpet with Bowyer as lead vocal. Managed by T.J. Byrne, the Royal Showband went professional in 1959 and toured the English Mecca Ballroom circuit in 1961 to great acclaim.

In April 1960, the *Munster Express* reported:

Waterford's Royal Showband currently hitting the high spots in England, will appear under a different name in a star-studded concert in Victoria Palace. The distinguished concert audience will include at least two members of the British Royal Family.

For this 'Royal' performance, the band must drop their now famous regal name and appear simply as – well probably – 'The Waterford Showband'.

The band's first No. 1 was 'Kiss Me Quick' in 1963, which stayed top of the charts for seven weeks. A documentary film was produced on the Royal in 1962, entitled 'The One Nighters', which was warmly received and saw an EP released with songs from the film. Their most enduring hit was the 'Hucklebuck' which sparked a dance craze reaching No. 1 in January 1965 and charted in the UK.

In 1968, the band had its first six-month residence in Las Vegas, and had its last performance in that city in July 1971, with the band breaking up.

VAL DOONICAN:
Crooner and Television Personality

Val Doonican born at 10 Passage Road, Waterford, and in 1927 was educated at De La Salle College. He went on to become a household name in Ireland, England and Australia through his music and television programmes. He was an admirer of Gene Autry and Roy Rogers. His first performances came at the Ballybricken Carnival to raise funds for the building of the Holy Family Church.

Doonican joined a couple of touring bands, such as Bruce Clarke's and the Four Ramblers, before coming to prominence on the BBC radio programme 'Riders on the Range'. At a birthday party for Anthony Newley it was suggested that the Waterford man's talents would be better showcased as a solo act. His big break came in 1963 when he had a spot on the TV show *Sunday Night at the London Palladium*. Doonican was booked by Val Parnell for an eight-minute slot which in his own words made him 'an overnight success after seventeen years'.

His record 'Walk Tall' became a big hit and a million-seller in 1964, and he went on to make over fifty albums. Having television shows for nearly 24 years, Doonican was a star of Saturday night television, and his Christmas Eve show became annual fare enjoyed by fans in Britain and Ireland. His appearance of a cardigan sitting in a rocking chair, with his crooner style, suited the season. Doonican's programme gave exposure to acts such as the comedian Dave Allen. Such was the former De La Salle student's popularity that his album *Val Doonican Rocks, But Gently* knocked the Beatles' *Sgt Pepper* off the top of the UK charts in 1968. Doonican was the subject of the *This Is Your Life* programme in 1970.

He died aged 88 in 2015.

GILBERT O'SULLIVAN:
Singer-Songwriter

Gilbert O'Sullivan was born Raymond O'Sullivan in 1948 at 18 O'Connell Street, Waterford, before moving to the Cork Road and emigrating to Swindon, England, aged 8. He was noticed by the manager of Engelbert Humperdink and Tom Jones, Gordon Mills, which led to him changing his name to Gilbert O'Sullivan. His hit songs include 'Alone Again (Naturally)', 'Clair' and 'Get Down'. The Irish singer has said that his music is in the 'English tradition'.

Court battles with his former manager over publishing rights, which O'Sullivan won, would prove damaging to his career, as he was portrayed as a bad guy. Another legal dispute arose in the 1980s when American rapper Biz Markie sampled 'Alone Again (Naturally)' without his permission. The issue was motivated by maintaining the artist's integrity and the right to ownership of his work as property rather than motivated by financial gain. As of 2018 he had recorded nineteen albums.

BOBBY CHARLTON AND WATERFORD FC

Charlton's time in the League of Ireland may have been brief but it left a lasting impression for fans of the Irish game. While for some of us, his Waterford ... career represents a fun pub trivia question, for others it was much more meaningful. For those who saw the great man in the flesh, his short time with the club was simply magical and last long in the memory.

Conor Patrick Heffernan, These *Football Times*, 8 January 2015

Bobby Charlton played 606 games for Manchester United and received 106 international caps for England. His honours included a FIFA World Cup in 1966, a European Cup in 1968 with his club team, as well as several leagues and cups. Charlton joined Preston North End in 1974 as player-manager but his first season in charge saw the Lancashire club relegated to the third tier of English football. His relationship with the board of the club soured over a proposed transfer of a player to Newcastle United. This led him to leave the club and join Waterford FC in the League of Ireland in 1976.

His signing for the Kilcohan club was announced after a 2–1 defeat to Limerick on 11 January 1976. The chairman of Waterford, Joseph Delaney, stated that the duration of Charlton's stay at the club depended on the support of fans, with increased gate receipts, and on other clubs sharing part of their takings when the Blues came to their grounds. The former Ballon d'Or winner's debut for the south-east club came against St Patrick's Athletic on 18 January which saw gate receipts nearly double at Kilcohan. He was pivotal in the centre of midfield in his side's 3–1 victory.

This was followed by another 3–1 victory against Finn Harps with 6,000 supporters in attendance. The former Manchester United player scored his first and only goal for the club and was deemed to be the fittest player on the pitch. The failure of Waterford to agree some share of gate receipts when travelling for away games led to difficulties in compensating Charlton. He played two more games for the club, both defeats away from home, 2–0 to Bohemians of Dublin in the league and 3–0 to Finn Harps in the cup.

He returned to England and had a brief spell with Wigan Athletic as a director and caretaker manager and later joined the board of former club Manchester United.

BARRY LYNDON:
The Making of a Cinematic Masterpiece

The historian Donald Brady considers *Barry Lyndon* to be 'without doubt the most important film ever produced in Waterford'. It was based on the novel *The Luck of Barry Lyndon* (published in 1844) by William Makepeace Thackeray and set in the eighteenth century, which was in turn based on the true story of Andrew Robinson Stoney, an Anglo-Irish soldier who tried but failed to climb English social circles. It was considered to be the first novel without a hero. The character of Lyndon is born in Ireland and rises through two armies to frequent the circles of British aristocracy. He is coldly calculating in his pursuit of rising from his humble beginnings. But this all falls apart when his loses his wife, fortune and even a leg (the latter a deviation from the original book).

Production for the film was initially based in Waterford, with Waterford Castle being used as a location. Filming began in 1973 under the directorial guidance of Stanley Kubrick after the release of *A Clockwork Orange* (which was withdrawn from British cinemas in 1973 in response to the film being responsible for copycat violence) and the failure to make a film about Napoleon.

Kubrick and his family would flee Ireland in January 1974 after he 'received a tip-off from the Gardaí that death threats had been made against him by the IRA'. It appeared that someone had not taken kindly to seeing the depiction of British soldiers (the backdrop being the Seven Years' War) being filmed in Ireland. Officially, however, the production company stated that his departure from the Emerald Isle was due to the filming schedule having finished there.

The cast included Ryan O'Neal (a Hollywood star after the success of the film *Love Story*) as the title character (the role was originally offered to Robert Redford but he declined) and former model Marisa Berenson played Lady Honoria. Filmed at Huntington Castle in Carlow, Cahir Castle, Powerscourt in County Wicklow and various locations in Waterford, the movie cost over $11 million to make. Academy Award nominations were received for Best Film and Best Director, winning in the categories of Cinematography, Art Direction, Costume Design and Musical Score in 1976. The renowned film critic Roger Ebert noted of the film that:

> The film has the arrogance of genius. Never mind its budget or the perfectionism in its 300-day shooting schedule. How many directors would have had Kubrick's confidence in taking this ultimately inconsequential story of a man's rise and fall, realizing it in a style that dictates our attitude toward it? We don't simply see Kubrick's movie, we see it in the frame of mind he insists on – unless we're so closed to the notion of directorial styles that the whole thing just seems like a beautiful extravagance (which it is). There is no other way to see Barry than the way Kubrick sees him.

Kubrick's filmography includes *Spartacus* (1960), *Dr Strangelove* (1964), *2001: A Space Odyssey* (1968), *A Clockwork Orange* (1971) and *The Shining* (1980).

WATERFORD LOCAL RADIO:
From Pirate Station to Licensed Operation

Rick Whelan and Egidio Giani laid the foundations for the development of Waterford Local Radio, which saw its first regular broadcast take place in 1978. It was transmitted from a garage in Butlerstown and broadcast from 10 a.m. to 6 p.m. Funds from advertising enabled them to increase their broadcast range to a 20-mile radius. After a year, Des Whelan was made station manager while Geoff Harris and Rick Whelan were among the early presenters for the station. The same year saw a clampdown on illegal or pirate radio stations which impacted the efforts in Waterford. Thanks to a back-up transmitter, they were back on air in just 4 minutes. It would prove to be one of the longest-lasting unlicensed pirate radio operations (closing in 1988 when the IRTC, later the Broadcasting Authority of Ireland, were issuing licences the following year).

At the end of 1979, they moved their production to a new location at Wellington Street in Waterford City. The 1980s saw increased popularity and provided an opportunity for burgeoning talent on air such as Billy McCarthy, Clodagh Walsh and Tony Weldon. The group's rebelliousness was demonstrated in their 1980 St Patrick's Day float, with members of the station dressing as pirates. Waterford Local Radio also had a social conscience and raised much-needed funds for the Lions Club with a well-supported Christmas appeal.

In 1989, Waterford Local Radio was the only pirate station to receive a local broadcasting licence, with popular presenters including Carrie Crowley, Timmy Ryan and Eddie Wymberry. Competition for this licence for Waterford came from Deise Broadcasting (previously ABC Radio which broadcast from Egans bar) and Waterford Radio. WLR FM broadcasted from studios in Georges Street before moving to a purpose-built premises at Ardkeen which is shared with Beat (since 2003) and a studio in Dungarvan.

INDUSTRY IN THE CITY:
Rise and Decline

The following is a brief look at some of the well-known factories that were substantial employers in Waterford City.

Clover Meats was originally called the Dead Meat Factory and was a pilot plant for the Irish Co-operative Organisation before being renamed in 1934. Based at Christendom, Ferrybank, the factory initially specialised in bacon, and later in beef killing, canning, cooking meats and the production of sausages. During the Second World War its canned products were popular in the United Kingdom. By 1961, the turnover for the factory was £6.9 million, as it developed the beef processing production of the plant. The end of the decade saw its turnover nearly double. Profits would dwindle over the course of the 1970s with a loss of £2 million in 1977. There was a brief reprieve in 1980 with the landing of a substantial contract but it closed in 1984 with the loss of nearly 500 jobs.

The Flourmills was situated on the North Wharf which encompassed the R&H Hall building, dating to 1889. It opened as the Flourmills in 1935, closing in 1977. The plant produced animal feed. Always at the forefront of technological innovation, going into the 1960s there was an oversupply of wheat in Ireland. Competition from foreign imports and recession in Ireland were major factors in the plant closing.

Waterford Iron Foundry opened in 1936 at Bilberry and in the following decade employed the most people in Waterford City. The factory specialised in black-painted graphite numbers and range cookers such as the Waterford Dover. There was a decline in production in the 1950s but the No. 3 and No. 40 Raeburn would see an upturn in fortunes, with the plant employing 600 people in the 1960s. The introduction of Waterford Colourcast cookware aided the company's success. There were a number of redundancies during the 1970s as sales declined, followed by the company entering receivership in 1982. In March of the following year, it was acquired by Frank Cruess-Callaghan and Owen Conway and renamed Waterford Stanley Limited. The creation of the Stanley Super-star cooker and a Twin Burner cooker saw the factory do well.

J. and L.F. Goodbody, known as the Jute Factory, was developed at a 5-acre site at Tycor provided by the Waterford Corporation. Building of the factory began in December 1936, with construction completed by March 1938. Initially staffed by 180 people, this rose to 600 at the height of production in the 1950s. Three-quarters of the workforce were women. In the early years, the factory produced up to 2.5 tons of jute a week. There was a brief closure during the Emergency in 1941 due to a lack of raw materials. The late 1950s saw the plant diversify into premium yarn for carpets to maintain its competitiveness. By 1958, the factory produced an average of 25 tons of jute cloth per week. Such cloth was used in the manufacturing of bags for potatoes and wheat or the backing for carpets. The 1970s saw the workforce of the factory reduced to 400. Due to lack of demand for the product, the factory eventually closed in 1974.

ACEC was established in 1951, based at Tycor with a workforce of between 150 to 200 people. The early 1980s saw small numbers of staff made redundant due to the perceived failure of investment from the plant's parent company in Belgium. The factory was bought by ABB Transformers and changed to the same name. It specialised in manufacturing for the construction and utility markets in Ireland and the United Kingdom. The operation in Waterford closed in 2010 with the loss of 178 jobs. At its closure it was based near Waterford Industrial Estate.

The National Board and Paper Mills, known as the Papermills, opened in 1952 and by 1959 employed up to 300 workers. It witnessed the longest strike action of a factory in Waterford when workers went on strike in March 1966, which lasted five months, in relation to changing the way shifts operated. By the middle of the 1970s the plant had a workforce of 500 people, but closed in 1978.

The Sack and Bag Company was established in 1955 and went on to become the largest producer of heavy-duty polythene sacks in Ireland but closed by the end of the 1960s.

Munster Chipboard was located on a 40-acre site in the centre of Waterford City at Tycor. It opened in 1962 and started with a staff of 150 people. An extension of the plant was completed in 1968, with the workforce increasing by 100 to increase production. However, issues related to dust with residents of Belvedere Drive, Lisduggan and Marian Park were not resolved satisfactorily. The factory closed in 1979 after entering receivership with mounting debts.

Kromberg and Schubert was the second largest employer in Waterford City, employing over 1,100 people by the mid-1990s. It operated from 1973 until Christmas 2004.

The paper and foil converting company Raytex was based at 'the Rock' before moving to a 15-acre site in Kilcohan. A new factory was opened in July 1980 and was employing 200 people. Gradual decline saw it close in early 1992, with 58 people made unemployed.

THE FALLOUT OF THE CELTIC TIGER, 2009–14

The 1990s saw major developments in the Irish economy, yet this appears to have led to little change in the landscape of Waterford City. Some changes included the creation of a nightclub quarter at John Street, the construction of City Square Shopping Centre at Arundel Square and the pedestrianising of the city centre into John Roberts Square. The construction of the Millennium Plaza yielded dividends, with the hosting of the Tall Ships in 2005. David Toms considers these developments to have 'merely papered over the cracks of the effects of de-industrialisation and regional neglect' which were amplified with the subsequent economic collapse of the national economy in 2008–09. The closure of the Waterford Crystal site at Kilbarry was one of the major falls of an icon during the recession.

Yet renewal came in the form of the Viking Triangle development and the House of Waterford Crystal on the Mall. It seems heritage and history have gone a long way to revitalising Waterford City. However, there were still industrial relations conflicts that saw workers from Europrice and The Park Inn stage sit-ins, and job losses at TalkTalk and Honeywell.

POPULATION FIGURES

POPULATION OF WATERFORD CITY			
YEAR	WATERFORD CITY[1]	COUNTY WATERFORD[2]	COUNTY WATERFORD CHANGE[3]
1831	28,821	176,898	
1841	28,439	196,187	
1851	31,499	164,035	(-32,152)
1861	28,623	134,252	(-29,783)
1871	28,959	123,310	(-10,942)
1881	28,950	112,768	(-10,542)
1891	27,507	98,251	(-14,517)
1901	27,372	87,187	(-11,064)
1911	28,079	83,966	(-3,221)
1926	27,215	78,562	(-5,404)
1936	28,553	77,614	(-948)
1946	_	76,108	(-1,506)
1951	29,235	75,061	(-1,047)
1956		74,031	(-1,030)
1961	28,719	71,439	(-2,592)
1966		73,080	1,641
1971	32,823	77,315	4,235
1979		87,278	9,963
1981	38,473	88,591	1,313
1986		91,151	2,560
1991	33,857	91,624	473
1996		94,680	3,056
2002	36,159	101,546	6,866
2006	45,748	107,961	6,415
2011	46,732	113,795	5,834

1 'Waterford Historical Mapping Tool', All-Island Research Observatory – National University of Maynooth [viewed 13-03-2019] http://airo.maynoothuniversity.ie/external-content/population-change-1841-2002-waterford

2 Central Statistics Office [viewed 15-12-2016] http://www.cso.ie/px/pxeirestat/statire/SelectVarVal/saveselections.asp

EPILOGUE

Our city centre is where it was when Strongbow was a boy, Patrick Street is as steep today as it was when Columbus discovered America in 1492 and we still enter Waterford from the north via a bridge built on the same line as Timbertoes, which was under construction when Wolfe Tone was organising the United Irishmen in Belfast. Time has changed Urbs Intacta but the charm that a thousand years of history has brought is enduring.

Eamonn McEneaney

*Wholly men know well
the way to heaven is as
good by water as is
by land —
standing here in the
harbour of the sun;
the as yet unconquered
city —*

*You the water-mouthed
talk on
taking with you in your way
the stories that will not wash
bleeding sounds into sentences
stories into mind.*

David Toms, 'Urbs Intacta Manet', 2015

The history of Waterford encompasses local idiosyncrasies and national issues and has seen the city come in to contact with international affairs, which makes it a fascinating place to learn and explore. The urban area that stands today would look like a different planet to the land on which the Vikings first set foot in establishing a settlement here. The various trends and fashions, from devotional practices in the Middle Ages to the consumption of alcohol in the nineteenth century, are reflected in many of the buildings which stand to this day.

Waterford's second golden age in the Georgian period still stands boldly in the architectural achievements of John Roberts. The nineteenth century saw Waterford men such as Thomas Francis Meagher and William Vincent Wallace traverse the world, and have an impact far beyond the River Suir. Giants of world history from English Kings to Oliver Cromwell, Frederick Douglass to Stanley Kubrick have connections to Ireland's oldest city in political and cultural spheres that many an outsider would not expect in the south-east part of the most western periphery of the continent of Europe.

The people of Waterford have never been content with their lot, whether it be the Anglo-Norman expansion of the city walls to those who crossed the Atlantic for seasonal work in Newfoundland. The many industries that have been established, succeeded and fallen is similar to the arc of life itself. Culinary inventions, such as the blaa or Denny's form of bacon curing, and technological innovations in shipbuilding and glass have seen the name of the city go around the world like the wind. But even though we have such a great history and are increasingly more aware of acknowledging it in an appropriate fashion, there are always things that slip through the cracks. To paraphrase the Irish poet Eavan Boland, we as a people are defined by what we forget.

For the noble parts and successes in the centuries of the existence of Waterford City, there have been fires which have burnt the city to the ground, plague and famine which have wiped out populations, to waves of migration out of economic necessity, yet Waterford endures. Over the centuries we have seen two bridges erected to span the Suir. But some would say we're not there yet. Dr Noel Browne of this city sought to have a healthcare system to cater for all needs effectively. But some would say we're not there yet. The lives of Mary Strangman, Rosamond Jacob and Sybil Connolly are signposts in the changing role of women in society. Their efforts in the medical, political and fashion worlds are a shining example of the journey undertaken for half the population. It has increasingly improved, but some would say we're not there yet.

It is a city which has exhibited royalist sympathies to nationalistic tendencies. In many respects it was a city state which sought to maintain its best interests whether it be through the efforts of figures such as James Rice, eleven-time mayor of the city, to John Redmond, the man who finally saw a Home

Epilogue

Rule Bill passed for Ireland. They were symptomatic of the times in which they lived; Rice's religiosity would be out of step with today's social media obsessed world. Redmond's pronouncement on joining the war effort in the early twentieth century would be abhorred today and has led to his legacy being much maligned. Of course, with hindsight we would all avoid pitfalls and failures. The history should be judged in the context of the times in which it happened, not through the lens in which we view it today.

Noted as *Parva Roma* – Little Rome – though, the majority of its inhabitants' faith was towards Rome there was a religious tolerance, and more importantly co-existence that many parts of the island would have hoped to achieve. A religious minority such as the Quakers have left an indelible mark on the city from its industry to education.

The city of Waterford continues to be enriched, be it with cultural festivals such as *Spraoi* to Waterford Walls and annual remembrance ceremonies such as the 1848 Tricolour Celebrations to the First World War. The cityscape is decorated with various monuments and the blue plaques of the Waterford Civic Trust. The Viking Triangle bustles with tourists from all over the world. Waterford Crystal is still a prominent icon of the city as it was in the middle of the twentieth century. It is attractive to Scandinavian, English and North American visitors for its connection with these regions.

Waterford can boast a mistress to a future king of England, the mother of a Hollywood *noir* writer and to be the home of the greatest daffodil grower in the world. The city is an eclectic mix which I hope is reflected in this book. It is a history of Waterford City and is certainly not an attempt to be *the* history of the city. Over the course of reading, hopefully one has come to more of an understanding of the history of the city from its notable personalities, landmark buildings and significant events.

The effort has been like charting the River Suir. The study serves as the mouth of the river as an entry point to the history of Waterford City; to record the main bends and turns as the significant events which have directed the development of Waterford; to note the waves – be they invasions or political and social developments as well as the tidal flow as in the highs and lows of the city's history. But there is more to be explored, researched and written. There are facets of our society to be explored as our understanding and vernacular grows, the best is yet to come. I for one cannot wait to witness it all unfold.

BIBLIOGRAPHY

An Introduction to the Architectural History of County Waterford, Department of the Environment, Heritage and Local Government, no date.

Bartlett, Thomas, *Ireland: a history*. Cambridge University Press, Cambridge, NY, 2010.

Bonaparte-Wyse, O., *The Issue of Bonaparte-Wyse: Waterford's Imperial Relations*. Waterford Museum of Treasures, Waterford, 2004.

Burnell, Tom, *The Waterford War Dead*, History Press Ireland, Dublin, 2010.

Byrne, N.J. (ed), *The Great Parchment Book of Waterford*, Irish Manuscripts Commission, Dublin, 2007.

Byrne, N., *The Waterford Leper Hospital of St Stephen and the Waterford County and City Infirmary*, Dublin, 2011.

Cowman, D. and Brady, D., *The Famine in Waterford 1845–1850*, Dublin Geography Publications in association with Waterford County Council, 1995.

de Courcy, J., *Ireland and the Irish in Maritime History*, Glendale Press, Dublin, 1986.

Dooley, Thomas P., *Irishmen or English Soldiers?: The Times and World of a Southern Catholic Irish Man (1876–1916) Enlisting in the British Army During the First World War*, Liverpool University Press, Liverpool, 1995.

Dowling, D., *Waterford Streets Past and Present*, Waterford Corporation, Waterford, 1998.

Downey, A., *The Glamour of Waterford*, The Talbot Press, Dublin, 1921.

Downey, E., *The Story of Waterford, From the Foundation of the City to the Middle of the Eighteenth Century*, Waterford News Printing Works, Waterford, 1914.

Dudley Edwards, Ruth with Bridget Hourican, *An Atlas of Irish History*, Routledge, London and NY, 2005.

Egan, P.M., *Historic Guide and Directory of County and City of Waterford*, Kilkenny, 1894.

Fayle, H. and Newham, A.T., *The Waterford and Tramore Railway*, Newtown Abbot, Devon, 1964.

Fewer, T.N., *Waterford People: a biographical dictionary*, Ballylough Books, Waterford, 1998.

Fitzpatrick, T., *Waterford during the Civil War 1641–1653*, Downey, Waterford, 1912.

Foster, R.F., *Modern Ireland 1600–1972*, Penguin, London, 1989.

Foster, R.F., *Vivid Faces: The Revolutionary Generation in Ireland, 1890–1923*, Penguin UK, London, 2014.

Fraher, W. and Ui Uallachain, P. *The Newfoundland Emigrant Trail*, Waterford County Museum, Waterford, 2010.

Hansard, J., *The History, Topography and Antiquities of the County and City of Waterford*, Dungarvan, 1870.

Inglis, H.D., *Ireland in 1834: a journey throughout Ireland during the Spring Summer and Autumn of 1834*, Whittaker, London, 1834.

Irish, B., *Shipbuilding in Waterford 1820–1882: a historical, technical and pictorial study*, Wordwell Ltd, Wicklow, 2001.

Bibliography

Kennedy, B., *Characters and Closures*, self-published, no date.

Keohan, E.D. (ed.), *Waterford City and Region: an historical and pictorial almanac of Waterford City and County*, Waterford, 1987.

Lane, Leeann, *Rosamond Jacob: Third Person Singular*, University College Dublin Press, Dublin, 2010.

Lee, J.J., *The Modernisation of Irish Society 1848–1918*, Gill and Macmillan, Dublin, 1989.

Lewis, S., *A Topographical Dictionary of Ireland*, 2 volumes, S. Lewis and County, London, 1837.

Long, Colm, *Random Waterford History*, self-published, Waterford, 2013.

Lyons, F.S.L., *Ireland since the famine*, Fontana, London, 1973.

McArdle, Dorothy, *The Irish Republic: a documented chronicle of the Anglo-Irish conflict and the partitioning of Ireland, with a detailed account of the period 1916–1923*, 3rd edn, Wolfhound Press, Dublin, 2005.

McCarthy, Pat, *The Irish Revolution, 1912–23: Waterford*, Four Courts Press, Dublin, 2015.

McElwee, R., *The Last Voyages of the Waterford Steamers*, Waterford Book Centre, Waterford, 1995.

McEneaney, E., *Discover Waterford*, O'Brien Press, Dublin, 2001.

McEneaney, E. (ed.), *A History of Waterford and its Mayors, from the 12th to the 20th century*, Waterford Corporation, Waterford, 1995.

McEneaney, E. (ed.), *Waterford Treasures*, Waterford, 2004.

Mackey, P., *Waterford Fireside Stories*, Waterford, 1989.

Murphy, John A., *Ireland in the Twentieth Century*, Gill and Macmillan, Dublin, 1975.

Nolan, William, and Thomas P. Power (eds.) *Waterford: History and Society: interdisciplinary essays on the History of an Irish County*, Geography Publications, Dublin, 1992.

O'Connor, Emmet, *A Labour History of Waterford*, Waterford Trades Council, Waterford, 1989.

O'Donoghue, F., with Andy Kelly, *Goin' to the Pictures*, self-published, no date.

O'Neill, J., *Waterford: a history*, Waterford, 1992.

O'Neill, J., *Waterford: its history and people*, Waterford, 2008.

O'Neill, J., *A Concise History of Waterford*, Waterford, 2011.

O'Neill, M. (ed.), *Reminiscences of Waterford*, Waterford, 1997.

Pender, S. (ed.), *Council Books of the Corporation of Waterford 1662–1700*, Irish Manuscripts Commission, Dublin, 1964.

Power, D., *The Ballads and Songs of Waterford*, Volume 1, Waterford, 1992.

Power, D., *The Street Where You Live*, Waterford, 1993.

Power, Patrick C., *History of Waterford City and County*, Mercier Press, Cork, 1990.

Russell, Ian and Maurice F. Hurley (eds.), James Eogan (executive editor), *Woodstown: a Viking Age settlement in County Waterford*, Four Courts Press, Dublin, 2014.

Ryland, R.H., *The History Topography and Antiquities of the County and City of Waterford, with an account of the present state of the peasantry of that part of the south of Ireland*, John Murray, London, 1824.

Sheridan, M., *Murder in Monte Carlo*, Poolbeg, Dublin, 2011.

Smith, C., *The Ancient and Present State of the County and City of Waterford*, 2nd edition, Wilson, Dublin, 1774.

Thackeray, W.M., *The Irish Sketch Book*, Smith Elder and County, London, 1887.
Walsh, J.E., *Ireland One Hundred and Twenty Years Ago*, Waterford, 1911.
Walsh, K. (ed.), *Waterford Memories, 150 years with the Munster Express*, Dublin, 2010.
Walton, J.C, *The Royal Charters of Waterford*, Waterford Corporation, Waterford, 1992.
Walton, Julian, O'Donoghue, Frank (ed.) *On This Day*, Vol. 1, Waterford, 2013.
Walton, Julian, O'Donoghue, Frank (ed.) *On This Day*, Vol. 2, Waterford, 2014.

NEWSPAPERS AND PERIODICALS

Ballybricken and Thereabouts, C.A.R.A, Waterford, 1991.
Cork Examiner.
Decies – the journal of the Waterford Archaeological and Historical Society, Vol. 1–74.
Irish Independent.
Irish Times.
Journal of the Waterford and South East of Ireland Archaeological Society, Vol. 1–18, 1895 to 1915.
Munster Express.
Waterford News.
Waterford Standard.
Waterford Star.

ONLINE SOURCES

Central Statistics Office, www.cso.ie/en/index.html
The Irish Story, www.theirishstory.com
Sidelines, thesidelinesofhistory.wordpress.com
Stair na hÉireann/History of Ireland, stairnaheireann.net
Waterford Harbour Tides and Tales, tidesandtales.ie
Waterford Treasures, waterfordtreasures.com